PRESENTATION

*Following the publication of our guide books
"Palazzo Farnese di Caprarola", "The Sacred Forest
of Bomarzo", "Bagnoregio and Civita", "Bolsena",
"Tuscania", "Villa Lante di Bagnaia",
"The Sanctuary of Santa Maria della Quercia",
"San Martino al Cimino and the Lake of Vico",
(all of which are available in English except the last three)
we now take pleasure in presenting this new volume
dedicated to the most important locality in the area
of Viterbese Tuscia, the capital city of the province, Viterbo.
Most of the guide books which have been written
about this city have been devoted chiefly to the fine
examples of architecture from its prestigious Medieval
phase while ignoring other aspects of Viterbo that are
of equal or greater interest for the tourist and which
include, not only its monuments and art works, but also
information about its hot springs, crafts and cuisine.
We are grateful to the local tourist board,
the* Azienda di Promozione Turistica
della Provincia di Viterbo
*for their invaluable assistance in the writing of the book,
and also wish to express our sincere thanks to the author,
Bruno Barbini whose readable and informative text
provide enjoyable and useful reading for the tourist.*

THE EDITOR

Bruno Barbini

VITERBO

HISTORY AND MASTERPIECES

132 Color Illustrations
Map of the city with the major points of interest

BONECHI EDIZIONI "IL TURISMO" FIRENZE

Agent and Distributor for Latium (excluding Rome):
Archidee (Claudio Tini)
Località Sant'Egidio
01032 Caprarola (VT)
Tel. and Fax 0761 647540

© Copyright 1999 by Bonechi Edizioni "Il Turismo" S.r.l.
Via dei Rustici, 5 - 50122 FIRENZE
Tel. +39-055.239.82.24/25 - Fax +39-055.21.63.66
E-mail: barbara@bonechi.com
         bbonechi@dada.it
http://www.bonechi.com

Photographs: Photo Archives of Bonechi Edizioni "Il Turismo" S.r.l.
              Paolo Bacherini
Cover: Claudia Baggiani
Revising of texts: Lorena Lazzari
Photolithographs: Bluprint srl. Firenze
Printer: BO.BA.DO.MA. Firenze

ISBN 88-7204-423-5

We wish to thank the creators of the "Machine of Santa Rosa", M. Andreoli, L. Cappabianca, and G. Cesarini for the loan of the picture which appears of page 48, taken by Foto Capulli.

VITERBO: A BRIEF HISTORY

The history of the city of Viterbo – or at least the part of it for which we have reliable information – begins in the Middle Ages. From the preceding era we have only a few ruins of ancient buildings and legendary versions of the origins of the city (fables in which characters from Classical mythology or from pre-Roman Italic traditions are combined with Old Testament figures, and often fused in an ingenuous mixture of pagan and Christian beliefs, just as occurred with Noah, who, having seen what the world was like both before and after the Flood, came to be identified with the two-faced Roman god, Janus). It is of course the ruins which constitute the only concrete proof that on the hill where the Cathedral and the Papal Palace were later built, and long before Rome came to dominate the territory, there must have been an Etruscan city which, though not very large, probably had a certain importance as a fortified area. Not only was this influence maintained after the Romans crossed over from the mysterious Forest of Ciminia in 310 BC and spread their dominion throughout Southern Etruria, but the strategic importance of the location actually increased during the second half of the next century, due to the construction of a consular road, the Via Cassia, which, even now, after many centuries, still constitutes the main thoroughfare crossing the province. According to local tradition the city perched on top of the hill, though it probably suffered considerable damage as it resisted the invasion of the Romans – continued to exist and the name Castello di Ercole (Castle of Hercules) which has come down to us would suggest the existence of a temple dedicated to the legendary Greek hero. This in fact must have been the ancient nucleus of the future city of Viterbo; for the other towns in the outlying areas, perhaps once even larger and more prosperous, we now have only the great necropoli or burial grounds to tell us of their existence and of their disappearance in a distant past.

After the decline of Roman power, the territory of Viterbo was first conquered by the Gauls, then by the Byzantines, the Lombards, the Franks, and finally became part of the original group of states subject to the temporal power of the Pope. At the beginning of the 9th century the area now occupied by the city consisted only of a few scattered villages (called vici*) and groups of houses which, as the population increased, grew together until the inhabitants of the Castello (which was by that time no longer called Castrum Herculis but Castrum Viterbii) began to move beyond the confines of the hill and started to build new houses in the countryside around it. The extension of the inhabited area probably began shortly after the year 1000; around the same time the new city organized itself as a free Comune and asserted its dominion within a territory which then came to be called Patrimonio di S. Pietro in Tuscia, or the Estates of St. Peter in Etruria- thus uniting the memory of its Etruscan origins with its new condition as a dominion of the Catholic Church, or Papal State.*

A series of historical events and political vicissitudes document Viterbo's growing power and authority in the Late Middle Ages. In fact, in 1145, during one of those periods in which social unrest and revolts made Rome particularly dangerous, Pope Eugene IV came to stay in Viterbo, which he deemed to be a quieter and safer seat for the papal

Preceding page: ***panorama of the city.***

power, and at this time conceived the idea of the Second Crusade which departed from the nearby town of Vetralla on December 1st of the same year.

In 1167 Viterbo was designated with the title of City by the Emperor, Frederick Barbarossa, to whom the citizens of Viterbo had granted assistance, one of the rare cases in the history of the city in which their consistent position of loyalty to the Pope was abandoned. In 1172 the long rivalry between Viterbo and Ferento finally came to an end. Ferento had been an important city in the Roman era, but after centuries of barbarian incursions it was little more than an impoverished hamlet. It was finally destroyed in order to avenge a series of betrayals, and in particular, an unexpected and particularly savage sack of Viterbo which the Ferentines had committed after having used a stratagem in order to get the men of the city to leave it undefended. Twenty years later Pope Celestine III appointed Viterbo a Bishopric.

The first half of the 13th century is typified by the participation of the city in the endless dispute between the Emperor, Frederick II of Swabia, and the Pope. Traditionally, Viterbo had always sided with the Guelph party (which supported the Pope), except for a small minority of Viterbese, led by the Tignosi and Cocco families, who supported the Emperor, and again on this occasion the city sided with the Church faction. For this reason, in 1243 Viterbo was subjected to a long siege by the armies of the Emperor. It was during this dramatic moment in the history of the city that, along with the vigorous reaction of the papal legate, Cardinal Raniero Capocci, some of the chroniclers of the time stated that the ardent faith of a young girl named Rosa helped to galvanize the resistance of the citizens of Viterbo; she was later canonized and became St. Rose of Viterbo, patron saint of the city.

The power of the Swabians began to decline in 1250 after the death of Frederick II; Manfred was slain in the Battle of Benevento and Corradino was beheaded by order of Charles of Anjou, the new sovereign of the Kingdom of Naples, whose family began to exert their political dominance throughout Italy at this time. Rome was torn by civil and political strife and the Popes had begun to look for a safer and more peaceful location for their headquarters within the territories under their dominion. Viterbo was one of the cities that aspired to this honor; in any case, it was certainly with these expectations in mind (which had been encouraged by the visits of Pope Alexander IV and Pope Urban IV) that the Capitano del Popolo, Raniero Gatti (member of a family originally from Brittany that had gained wealth and power in Viterbo and become leaders of the Guelph party) had a magnificent palace built in 1255-1266. It is in this palace that Clement IV ended his papacy. His death gave rise to one of the longest periods of vacancy of the papal office: almost three years of negotiations and political maneuvers, carried on during what is generally considered the first Conclave in the history of the Church.

This event marks the period which is generally considered the most glorious moment in the history of the city. After Gregory X, whose election to the papacy finally put an end to the interregnum, Popes John XXI, Nicholas III and Martin IV were also elected in Viterbo. On account of the riots which occurred during the Conclave of 1281 in which Martin IV was elected, the new Pope placed the city under an interdict. From the end of the 13th century and for all of the follow-

Opposite: **Walls of the city.**

Part of the medieval quarter with the tower of the Palazzo del Podestà.

ing one, Viterbo was torn by bloody struggles between opposing political factions and different social classes led by the most powerful families of the city: the Gatti, the Tignosi and the Di Vico, while the absence of the Popes, who were now established in Avignon, made it difficult for them to impose papal authority. In the 14th century one noteworthy attempt in this direction was made by Cardinal Egidio Albornoz who in 1354 ordered the construction of the fortress which still bears his name.

The return of the Papacy to Italy from Avignon marked the beginning of the consolidation of the political power of the States of the Church and a period of relative peace and tranquility for the city of Viterbo. During this time the city was able to obtain numerous concessions and privileges from the popes and other powerful prelates; Pope Paul III, who was probably born in Viterbo and certainly spent part of his childhood there, took a particular interest in the city, as did his nephew Cardinal Alessandro Farnese.

This long and uneventful period of peace in Viterbo and the Papal estates comes to an abrupt end as a result of the political turmoil caused by the arrival in Italy of the French Revolutionary Armies; the traditional political structure of the States of the Church was replaced by new Republican ordinances and Viterbo became the capital of the Dipartimento di Cimino, and later, under the Napoleonic Empire, lost for the first time its autonomy as a province and was reduced to the modest role of capital of the Circondario, meaning that it maintained only minor administrative functions. The city became the administrative headquarters of the Estates of St. Peter in Tuscia again only after the Congress of Vienna and maintained its title of Provincial Capital even during the brief period of government by the Roman Republic in 1849. Garibaldi's troops liberated the city in 1860 and 1867, but these were isolated episodes which lasted only a few days, after which papal authority was restored. Unification with the new state of Italy became a reality only on September 12th 1870 when the city was taken by a division of the troops which, just eight days later, captured the city of Rome after gaining entrance through the famous gap blown open in the Porta Pia. A month later on October 15th, almost all of the territory of the region of Lazio was aggregated under the provincial authority of Rome and Viterbo again lost its title as a capital city, a title which it did not regain until 1927. The most dramatic events in the recent history of the city are those related to the Second World War, and in particular, between 1943 and the arrival of the Anglo-American troops on June 8th 1944, when Viterbo was almost continually under bombing attacks. The great loss of human life and massive destruction inflicted on the city were officially recognized in 1959 when the city received special recognition for the terrible damage suffered during the war.

Piazza del Plebiscito.

THE THREE CENTERS OF CIVIC LIFE

Modern Viterbo now of course has extended far beyond the city walls which once encompassed it, but the characteristics of the streets and buildings of the historic downtown area still maintain alive and unaltered the memory of a far distant but not forgotten past.

The best starting point for a visit to the city is from the **Piazza del Plebiscito** (Plaza of the Plebiscite) which was already the administrative center of the city starting in the second half of the 13th century. The buildings which house the city judicial authorities are built around this plaza: the most important of these is the Palazzo dei Priori. The portico of the Palazzo has stylistic similarities with the 13th century one in the Palazzo Alessandri (which will be discussed below), and this fact convinced scholars that it should be dated to the second half of the 13th century, while in reality construction was begun only in the second half of the 15th century, as is demonstrated by the great coat-of-arms of Pope Sixtus IV della Rovere on the façade. Work continued on the Palazzo for more than a century; in fact the gardens in back and the north wing were added only in the first decades of the 17th century. The second story of the Palazzo consists of a series of majestic halls which the municipal government uses for assemblies. The **Sala Regia** is the one of the most interesting of these rooms; it is decorated with frescoes painted around the end of the 16th century by Baldassare Croce which illustrate mythological and historical events relating to the history of Viterbo, starting with its legendary founding and including personages and events of the Middle Ages and Renaissance. On the ceiling, Tarquinio Ligustri and Ludovico Nucci painted scenes showing towns and castles within the dominions of Viterbo. In the garden of the Palazzo is a beautiful 18th century fountain built according to a design by Filippo Caparozzi.

Palazzo dei Priori.

Palazzo dei Priori, external courtyard;
on the right: ***Palazzo dei Priori, Sala Regia.***

On the right side of the façade, above the arch which crosses over one of the four access roads leading into the plaza, there is a corridor which connects the Palazzo dei Priori with the Palazzo del Podestà where the Municipal government has its offices. The slender 143 ft. tower which rises above the Palazzo was built over a pre-existing one in 1487. On the other side of the plaza the Palazzo del Capitano del Popolo is located. The building was radically remodeled in 1771 in order to make it into the residence of the Apostolic delegate and retains almost nothing of its original aspect. It now houses the offices of the Prefecture. On one of the corners of this building and of the **Palazzo del Podestà** there are ancient columns which support statues of lions sculpted in *nenfro*, a local volcanic stone which the Etruscans had used as one of their main building materials.

The fourth side of the plaza is occupied by a building which was used as a prison and by the **Church of Saint Angelo of Spatha** which was already in existence at the end of the 11th century, but was totally transformed in the 18th century so that it now looks completely different from the original. On the façade, to the right of the door, there is a Roman sarcophagus with bas-relief sculptures of hunting scenes, which is known as the *tomb of Galiana*, a young girl whose great beauty was the cause of her death. According to the legend, a Roman noble who had been scorned by Galiana laid siege to the city with the intent of taking her by force. Finally he consented to abandon the siege if he could lay eyes on her just once more, but when Galiana appeared on the top of the tower, he couldn't bear the idea that he was going to lose her forever and shot her down with an arrow. The sarcophagus has been severely damaged by pollution and weather and was removed several years ago from

Palazzo del Capitano del Popolo,
now the Prefecture.

the façade where it will be replaced by a copy. The original has been restored and placed in the Civic Museum.

The little church of **Santa Maria della Salute** is an original example of 14th century architecture and brings to mind the philanthropic activity of a wealthy notary of Viterbo, Master Fardo di Ugolino, who had ordered and paid for its construction around 1320, next to another building which he had had built as a shelter for wayward girls. We do not know if the noble intents of the notary ever reached their objective, but they did have the merit of promoting the creation of this distinguished little church with its four-lobed shape, a fine little tabernacle decorating one of the minor apses, and the main doorway with its elegant bas-relief decoration representing the Acts of Mercy. In view of the quality of the architecture, it is surprising that the tombstone in the floor of the little church, covering the place where Master Fardo was buried in 1348, was executed in such a crude manner.

Walking from Piazza del Plebiscito to Piazza San Lorenzo the visitor can see the way in which the burgeoning city began to expand during the 11th-13th centuries and how, as it grew, the center of the city was moved progressively outward following the line traced by this roadway. The two plazas are separated by only a few hundred yards, but all of the most important aspects and memories of the history of Viterbo are crowded together in the brief space in between.

One aspect typical of Viterbo is the layering in the same place of structures and artifacts of very different eras. This fact becomes apparent as we follow this essentially Medieval itinerary: on a side street we come upon the 15th century Palazzo Chigi with its courtyard adorned by an elegant portico. Slightly onward, we find ourselves in Piazza del Gesù where the city government was located in simple buildings when Viterbo established itself as a free Commune in the 11th century. Nothing remains of these ancient municipal government buildings except the portico where the Podestà administered justice, the outline of which is still visible in the wall of the Palazzo in the corner, on the left side of the plaza.

Lion carved in volcanic stone on top of an ancient column located at the corner of the Palazzo del Podestà.

On the left: *the austere architecture of Palazzo Chigi.* On the right: *Piazza del Gesù and the church of the same name.*

The Burgundian foot, an ancient unit of measurement carved into the base of the tower called the Torre del Borgognone.

On the other side of the plaza the visitor can admire the massive 13th century tower called the **Torre del Borgognone**. It would seem that the municipal authorities had decided to use the length of the foot of a certain Messer Angelo known as the Burgundian (Borgognone) as an official unit of measurement and the outline of the foot was chiseled on to the base of the tower. In 1243, as the armies of Frederick II tried in vain to break the resistance of the Viterbese, in the plaza a bloody battle took place between the faction loyal to the Emperor and that loyal to the Pope.

The **Chiesa del Gesù** (Church of Jesus), originally dedicated to St. Sylvester, whose simple facade faces on to the end of the plaza, was the scene of a particularly ferocious crime. On March 31st 1271, two French noblemen, Guido and Simone di Monfort decided to revenge the death of their father (who had been defeated in the Battle of Eversham and barbarously put to death by order of Edward I of England) by murdering young Henry of Cornwall, cousin of the English king, who happened to be in Viterbo with the retinue of Charles of Anjou and they attacked the young prince suddenly during the mass. Henry fled toward the altar in search of safety but was murdered on the spot along with the two deacons who had tried to defend him. This particularly cruel murder provoked a reaction of general horror and indignation which was expressed by Dante in his *Inferno*, where he places Guido among the sinners who committed acts of violence towards others, but in isolating him from his fellow sinners, accentuates the feelings of outrage felt toward a crime committed "in the arms of God". The existence of the church of St. Sylvester is recorded in documents as early as 1080 and the Romanesque lines of the façade clearly belong to this original structure, though there are indications of later remodeling and alterations throughout the building. The provincial tourist promotion association and a local bank, the Cassa di Risparmio, sponsored the restoration of the

Below: *Church of Gesù, detail of bell-tower;* to the right: *Piazza del Gesù and the Torre del Borgognone.*

Piazza della Morte, a characteristic feature of Viterbese architecture, the profferlo (a stairway connected to an arched balcony); to the left: Piazza della Morte, another architectural element typical of Viterbo, the spindle fountain.

church a few years ago, and it is now used for concerts, exhibitions and other cultural manifestations.

As we continue our walk toward what is considered to be the first inhabited area of the city of Viterbo, we come upon three particularly interesting monuments. The first of these is the fountain in the **Piazza della Morte** (the Plaza of Death), which is of a type called *fontana a fuso* or spindle-shaped fountain, a unique feature of Viterbese architecture. There are several of these fountains scattered throughout the city in various plazas and with more or less refined decorations on the sides of the pools and the central shaft, but they all have the same basic spindle design with a flower-shaped cusp on top, which, according to Appolonj Ghetti is the continuance of a decorative element which is found on Etruscan monuments in the area. The fountain was originally built in 1206 and rebuilt in the second half of the century after it had been destroyed in 1243 by a mob along with the nearby houses belonging to the Tignosi family (who, as mentioned, were leaders of the Ghibelline faction in the city) during the political struggles which took place in Viterbo in the 13th century. Proceeding toward the old city center, at the beginning of the bridge which leads to Piazza San Lorenzo, we find the Loggia di San Tommaso, which is named after a nearby church, now closed. In the 11th century the Tignosi family had had a structure built that would enable them to control the bridge and the loggia underneath served as an assembly hall. In the 12th century the building became the property of the Abbey of St. Martin, and later of the lay canons of the Cathedral who used it as a stopping place for the Bishop during religious processions. Afterwards it came in to the hands of a confraternity, the Confraternita dell'Orazione e Morte, the portico was walled up, and re-opened only a few years ago. After it was restored the portico was closed in with panes of glass and the rooms thus obtained are now used in the Summer season as an office for dis-

Below: *Piazza della Morte, San Bernardino preaching to the people of Viterbo.*

Piazza San Lorenzo and the Papal Palace; to the right: *Palazzo Farnese.*

Opposite page: *The cathedral with its Gothic bell-tower (14th century).*

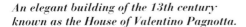

An elegant building of the 13th century known as the House of Valentino Pagnotta.

pensing tourist information. On the upper stories there is an interesting museum, the *Museo delle Confraternite.*

Beyond the bridge, on the right, the visitor can admire an imposing 15th century structure, the Palazzo Farnese, which was built by an ancestor of Pope Paul III. The building was restored to its original appearance in 1933 when most of the area was being rebuilt. Many typically medieval architectural elements are still visible; of particular interest are the windows which open out on to the side of the building, arranged in two registers of biforus windows inside a Gothic arch on the lower level and inside a round arch on the upper level. The stairway built against the wall of the courtyard is based on the types being used several centuries earlier.

The **Plaza of San Lorenzo** is located on top of the hill where there was once an Etruscan village, of which almost nothing remains, only a few crudely squared off stone blocks at the base of the bridge which joins the hill to the rest of the city and a few other ruins which have been covered over or built in to later structures. When these were built the area had already become periphery because the formation of the land which had earlier seemed a desirable location (due to the rise in the terrain which made it easy to defend) in the centuries which followed tended to direct the expansion of the city in a single direction. Several attempts were made to avoid or slow down this inevitable process, and even appeals were made to the religious sentiment of the populace, for example, in 1336 when the Bishop, Angelo Tignosi, issued an ordinance intended to reserve special privileges for the Cathedral by making it the only church in the city where it was possible to buy indulgences.

At the entrance to the plaza, described by Apollonj Ghetti as one of the most inspiring churchyards in Italy, it is possible to see a truly elegant example of 13th century civil architecture, the **House of Valentino della Pagnotta**, which has recently been restored to its original appearance after the damages caused by bombs during the last war.

Piazza San Lorenzo, a spindle fountain;
Below: *detail of the bell-tower and
the façade of the cathedral.*

Similar remodeling has been carried out on the **Cathedral** in order to restore its original Romanesque appearance. The cathedral was built between the 12th and 13th centuries in the location where the ancient parish church of San Lorenzo once stood and underwent profound alterations in the 16th and 17th centuries. The most apparent of these is the façade, which Cardinal Gambara had built in 1570 as a replacement for the earlier one, and which, in style, clashes with all the surrounding buildings. Inside the Cathedral, during the restorations carried out immediately after the war, all of the side chapels were closed off (as they were completely extraneous to the original structure), the central apse was rebuilt (it had been demolished by order of Cardinal Gambara in 1560 in order to make room for a vast and sumptuous choir) and the cross vaults of the ceiling were eliminated (they had been built by order of Bishop Brancacci in 1861 in order to cover the original truss and beam ceiling). In 1369 along with other construction work ordered by Pope Urban V the handsome *bell-tower* was built; its square shape and decoration with stripes in alternating colors reveal a Tuscan influence.

Cathedral, interior. *The Savior giving*
His Blessing, painting attributed
to Gerolamo da Cremona;
to the left: *Central nave of the Cathedral.*

Inside the church, along with numerous 17th and 18th century paintings (including several by the Viterbese painter Giovanni Francesco Romanelli who worked for many years at the French court), the following are of particular interest: *Redentore benedicente* (the Savior giving his blessing) dated 1472 attributed by most scholars to Gerolamo da Cremona (though it is attributed by some to Mantegna), and a *Madonna with Child*, formerly in the Church of Santa Maria in Carbonara, dated to the second half of the 12th century. Many scholars have pointed out the analogies that exist between this painting and the venerated image of the Madonna in the Basilica of Santa Maria Maggiore in Rome, for which the painting in Viterbo – according to Volbach – was the model. Several funeral monuments have been built in the Cathedral over the centuries: unfortunately the one which marked the tomb of Pope Alexander IV, buried here in 1261, is no longer in existence. However, at the beginning of the left nave, where it is now placed after having been moved from two earlier locations within the Cathedral, the visitor may observe the tomb of the only Portuguese pope, John XXI, who died in Viterbo in 1277 as a consequence of the collapse of a room in the nearby Papal Palace.

This building, **the Papal Palace**, was built between 1255 and 1266 by

Baptismal font
by Francesco da Ancona (1470). The base
and temple were later additions.

The Papal Palace with its great stairway (1267); on the right: *the Papal Palace.*

*Papal Palace,
detail of the façade.*

order of the Capitano del Popolo, Raniero Gatti and completes the awe-inspiring series of structures which frame the plaza. The lacy loggia, which has almost become the symbol of the city of Viterbo, was built in 1267 by Andrea di Berardo Gatti, nephew of Raniero. The building of this Palazzo was a concrete expression of Viterbo's desire to offer a quiet and dignified residence to the popes. The first pope to live there was Clement IV who was elected in Perugia and arrived in Viterbo in 1266. After he died two years later, neither of the two factions which had formed in the Sacro Collegio, the body which elects the pope, (a pro-Anjou faction supporting a French candidate and a pro-Imperial faction supporting an Italian candidate) were able to win the majority necessary for the election of a new pope. On this occasion, along with political personalities like Charles of Anjou and religious figures like St. Bonaventure of Bagnoregio who tried to find a solution to the deadlock, the city of Viterbo reacted with determination under the leadership of Raniero Gatti and two Podestàs, Corrado di Alviano and Alberto di Montebuono who locked up the cardinals *cum clave* (with a key, hence the term Conclave) in the room where the voting was taking place, rationed their food, and paid no attention whatever to the threats of excommunication made by the cardinals against not only the leaders but all the citizens of Viterbo; the expression used to date a letter of June 8th 1270 would seem to confirm the story that they even removed the roof of the hall in order to leave the cardinals without shelter from the weather and convince them to come to an agreement. In fact, pope Gregory X who was elected after almost three years of negotiations, accepted and promoted many of the rules which the exasperation of the citizens of Viterbo had suggested in the constitution "Ubi periculum" which was promulgated during the Council of Lyon in 1274 in order to establish a series of guidelines to regulate the activities of the Conclave.

*Loggia of the Papal Palace; detail
of the seven entwined arches with coats-
of-arms and relief carvings on the cornice;
on the left: general view of the loggia.*

*Loggia of the Papal Palace,
detail of the seven entwined arches
with coats-of-arms and bas-relief
carvings on the cornice.*

*Loggia of the Papal Palace,
a cardinal's coat-of-arms.*

The fountain of the loggia of the Papal Palace.

The spacious hall which is named for the first Conclave in the history of the Church can be reached through the door located at the top of the stairway outside. On the right side of the hall is the entrance way to the loggia; this is a structure of great elegance and refinement whose stability however was seriously compromised by the open fretwork over the arches because the slender coupled columns were not strong enough to support the entablature and the thrust from the eaves of the roof. Only a few decades after it was built in fact the back part of the loggia was already ruined and the front part, facing the plaza, was saved by filling in all of the empty spaces. At the beginning of this century, when the building was being restored and later additions were being removed, the use of modern construction techniques made it possible to open up the arches again by inserting a beam of reinforced concrete under the entablature. In the center of the loggia there is a fountain which recalls the construction of an aqueduct in 1268. Of the original structure only the upper basin and part of the column remain; the rest of it was built about two centuries later, as can be deduced by the presence of coats-of-arms of late 15th century popes and bishops carved on the base.

One of the oldest monuments in Viterbo is the bell-tower of the **Church of Santa Maria della Cella** which is located near the loggia on the side which overlooks the valley. This building complex once included a convent which was dependent on the Benedectine Abbey at Farfa and is mentioned in documents as early as the 8th century. The buildings were seriously damaged in an earthquake in 1349 and later abandoned and left in ruins. Only the bell-tower remains and has been recently restored in consideration of its particularly interesting architectural features. Its archaic elements, in fact, like the tapering columns and the trapezoid shaped capitals have analogies in other ruins of ancient buildings like the Lombard cloister of Santa Maria Nuova and the little bell-tower which stands in the oldest part of San Sisto.

The Papal Palace, the fountain of the loggia with the Sanctuary of Maria SS. Liberatrice in the background.

MEMORIES OF A FAR-GONE ERA
IN THE HOUSES OF SAN PELLEGRINO

According to an ancient chronicler of Viterbo, who was certainly more inclined to relate sensational news than carefully check his sources, the church which once stood where **Santa Maria Nuova** is now located was founded in 380 by the descendants of Hercules. Aside from the imaginary details of the story, it is quite probable that a sacred building stood here earlier; it is dated by Scriattoli to the 6th century on the basis of the decoration of a marble fragment which is now inserted in the side wall of the present day building. Another indication of the great antiquity of the ancient church is to be found in the features of the cloister which had almost completely disappeared as portions of it were covered with earth, with other structures and with additions of various types. Thanks to restoration work which at the time of this writing was still going on, the ancient cloister has almost completely regained its original appearance. Besides the cloister, the church had also been defaced by remodeling and alterations especially in the 16th century, and has now been returned to its original structure by restoration work which began in 1907 and went on for more than fifty years.

Façade of the Church of Santa Maria Nuova.

A *marble cippus* or marker located inside to the left of the main door informs us of the date of foundation of the church: in fact, carved on the stone is the text of the parchment document with which, in the year 1080, the priest Biterbo who promoted its construction, made a gift of it to the city along with the building, no longer extant, attached to it, which was used as a hospice for pilgrims. This took place at the beginning of Viterbo's period as a free Commune and the church (which was just a few yards away from the plaza of St. Sylvester where the buildings of the magistrates were located) probably offered a better guarantee of safety with respect to the humble buildings where the governors carried on their activity. This fact would explain why, besides its religious functions, for a certain period of time, the church was also used to store public funds and important documents, and was where the citizens of Viterbo held assemblies to discuss important problems of mutual interest. A carved inscription reminds us that from the pulpit, located on the left corner of the façade, St. Thomas Aquinas preached in 1266. The three apses located at the other end of the church reveal the influence of Lombard architecture and relate Santa Maria Nuova with other important monuments in Tuscia, like the famous Basilica of St. Peter in Tuscania.

Santa Maria Nuova.
Left corner of the façade,
the pulpit used by
St. Thomas Aquinas (1266).

The inside of the church, divided into three naves, is a beautiful example of Romanesque architecture which presents many stylistic analogies with the Cathedral. This similarity is accentuated by the detail of the capitals, each with a different type of ornament. On the walls of the church are frescoes dated from 1293 (the date is written below the anonymous *Crucifixion* located in the right nave) to the late 16th century, like the fresco of Saint Jerome in a niche located in the left nave. Among the various paintings, of particular interest are: the two *Crucifixions*: the one in the left nave which has recently been attributed by Faldi to Matteo Giovannetti of Viterbo (first half of the 14th century), and the other one, directly opposite, which is believed to be the work of another local painter, Francesco d'Antonio, called Il Balletta.

*Santa Maria Nuova,
the Lombard cloister,
one of the oldest monuments in Viterbo.*

A painting that is particularly venerated is the triptych representing the *Savior giving His blessing, between the Madonna and Saint John,* with *Saints Peter, Paul and Michael* on the external panels. Though this work was originally thought to be of the 4th or 5th century, scholars now agree that it must be 13th century. According to an ancient manuscript, the painting was found miraculously in 1283 when the crate which held it was hit by a plow and the oxen suddenly kneeled down and refused to continue plowing. It is likely that the triptych was buried in 1243 when the soldiers of Frederick II were laying siege to the city and using the wooden panels of paintings to make shields.

Another important monument that has recently been restored is the **Lombard Cloister**. Only two sides have been recovered as the other two had totally disappeared due to later additions, alterations and demolition. Along with the bell-tower of Santa Maria della Cella and San Sisto, with which it has evident analogies in its architectural elements, the Lombard Cloister is one of the oldest monuments in the city. The restoration of the cloister which restored the two sides now visible also brought to light the impressive *crypt.*

Not far from the church of Santa Maria Nuova, we come upon the

On this page: ***Neighborhood of San Pellegrino (the Medieval quarter) with its typical 'profferli.'***

Opposite: ***Piazza Cappella, another area typical of the Medieval quarter of Viterbo, with its unique 'profferlo' stairway.***

neighborhood (*quartiere*) of **San Pellegrino** and in doing so we enter a world of the past which offers to the eyes of the visitor a vision of things as they were six or seven centuries ago. This is not just a single building but a whole extraordinary urban setting in which houses and streets have maintained exactly the same appearance as they had in the Middle Ages. The visitor should walk along the main street of the *quartiere* which runs along its entire length and stop in the picturesque little squares in order to admire the architectural and decorative details of the buildings which seem to be suspended in time.

Strolling along the streets of San Pellegrino it is possible to observe many examples of what is considered the most typical element of the architecture of Viterbo, the **profferlo**. This is an external stairway leading to a balcony standing in front of the doorway to the house on the second story. The whole structure is supported by a round archway with a parapet on the side which is usually decorated with geometric motifs often of great elegance. The *profferli* are built with the same stone used for the walls of the houses, a rock of volcanic origin called *peperino* which is typical of this region. The different tones of gray which are characteristic of this stone are the dominant colors of the old civic center and give even the buildings with fancy decorations an appearance of severe simplicity. In the center of this neighborhood is the **Plaza of San Pellegrino** where we find the church of the same name and the **Palazzo degli Alessandri** which was the residence of a powerful family allied with the Gatti family who were not only relations but fellow members of the Guelph political party. This interesting building combines Gothic structural elements with others typical of the local tradition which makes it possible to date it to a period of transition, probably around the first half of the 13th century. This means that the palazzo must have been in existence for just a few years when, in 1251, the Ghibelline faction came temporarily to power and forced the leaders of the rival Guelph faction, including members of the Alessandri family, to flee from the city. There was a real danger that the new palazzo might be destroyed by the mob and it is extraordinary that the pope himself, Innocent IV, took the necessary steps to avoid just such an eventuality and from his residence in Perugia sent a Brief to the citizens of Viterbo ordering them to leave the building and its tower untouched.

In this splendid palazzo there is an unusual variant of the *profferlo*. The stairway in fact is not built against the external wall of the building but is built within a space formed by the perimeter walls of the palazzo itself and receives light from a balcony surmounted by a great round arch. The main body of this palazzo is connected to the building facing the church (which is built above a handsome portico) by a corridor above a rampant arch built over the street.

We are reminded of the ownership of the palazzo by the Alessandri family and their privileged position in the neighborhood by the numerous images of their coat-of-arms with the vair motif and cross of St. Andrew on the capitals of the columns and walls of nearby buildings. The Palazzo is now the property of the Provincial Administration which uses it for art exhibitions and other cultural manifestations.

The **Church of San Pellegrino** is first mentioned in documents of

*Church of San Pellegrino, fresco
on the outside of the left nave;
Church of San Pellegrino, façade.*

the 11th century where it is said that it depended on the Abbey of Farfa. This fact is easily explained if one considers that, until the middle of the next century, this great Sabine monastery possessed the adjacent area of Vico Squarano which was sold to the Commune of Viterbo in 1148 in order to permit the further expansion of the town. Every trace, however, of the original structure has been canceled by the alterations made in later eras and in particular the remodeling of the façade which was ordered and paid for by Bishop Grasselli at his own expense in 1889. This generous gesture unfortunately was not accompanied by an equivalent amount of good taste, and in accordance with the Bishop's orders the façade was redone in a Gothic style which clashes with the style of the surrounding buildings, and in the opinion of Apollonj Ghetti, was "a sour note" in the otherwise harmonious group of constructions on account of its "rude Gothic features".

*Left: **Archways in the Medieval quarter;**
above: **the little Plaza of San Pellegrino,
heart of the Medieval quarter.
The access to the plaza is covered
by an arch which connects the two wings
of the 13th century Palazzo which
belonged to the powerful Alessandri family.***

For a long time the neighborhood of San Pellegrino was inhabited almost entirely by peasants and laborers and over the centuries this fact determined a certain process of adaptation of the ancient houses to suit the needs of those living in them. For example, the arches supporting many of the *profferlo* were walled up in order to obtain a closed space which could be used as a storeroom or for other purposes connected with the work of the people who lived there, and not surprisingly, damages caused by use and time were repaired in a way which certainly did not respect the original structures. In these past few decades however a great deal has been done to try to return to their original appearance the houses which had been transformed and to consolidate the ones which were in danger of collapsing. The sheds and stalls have been turned into attractive shops and antique stores, and artists have located their studios in many of the ancient houses of the neighborhood. In this way the quarter of San Pellegrino has been able to avoid assuming the cold and lifeless appearance of a neighborhood which is preserved as a historical artifact with the sole purpose of recalling a distant past, and has found another, better way to maintain the ancient buildings respecting their original forms by using them as tourist attractions and shops which offer for sale a wide variety of typical local craft objects, valuable antiques and simple souvenirs.

This neighborhood in fact represents the ideal place for promoting and developing crafts and artistic activities which along with others in the field which are less attractive though just as useful, represent strong points in the economies of cities like Viterbo which have not yet been involved in an authentic industrial expansion.

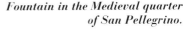

*Fountain in the Medieval quarter
of San Pellegrino.*

This page: ***two scenes showing the craft market in the Medieval quarter of San Pellegrino.***

A DIFFERENT KIND OF SHOPPING

Fifty or a hundred years ago the people of Viterbo made a distinction between artisans and other kinds of workers, in particular those who worked in the fields, and qualified the craftsmen as 'artists'. We must admit that in most cases this was no exaggeration. Nowadays the followers of this centuries-old tradition, though not so numerous as they once were, maintain the name of local craft products at the highest level by creating particularly refined and tasteful objects and practicing the art of restoration with patience and precision. Many of these workshops are located in the ancient houses of the San Pellegrino quarter, where the visitor can find objects that are truly different from the mass produced pseudo-souvenirs so often found in similar tourist attractions, which, as they are totally impersonal and have eliminated all of the unique local features, merely represent the monotonous standardization unfortunately so typical of our era.

The city and the province of Viterbo both have ancient and prestigious craft traditions. Even though the desire for lighter work and higher pay often turn young people away from these activities, here we can still find expert *maestri* who are true artists in their trade; particularly worthy of mention are the stone masons, many of whom are real sculptors. The restorations made necessary after the last war which required the creation of many architectural elements which had been completely destroyed and the constant maintenance of the artistic heritage of the city which often requires the substitution of pieces which have been damaged beyond repair are a clear demonstration of the amazing capacity of these artisans to cross over the confines separating craft from art. Besides stonemasonry, other important craft activities are wrought iron and leatherwork, furniture restoration, the creation of luxury furniture and objects with wooden inlay decoration called *intaglio*, and the production of art pottery and traditional objects made of earthenware. The narrow picturesque rooms which open out directly on to the roadway are the ideal environment for the promotion and appreciation of activities such as these for which ancient traditions and the necessity of a direct manual activity by man during the production process give a special meaning in a world which is now totally conditioned by the impersonal characteristics typical of mass production.

Not only is San Pellegrino the ideal environment for the production of artistic and craft objects, it is also, of course, the perfect place for holding manifestations recalling ancient times. This particular neighborhood, like others where the Medieval past is particularly felt, is often the stage for historical and folkloristic re-enactions which are also occasions for contests with groups from other cities with similar traditions. Among the most popular events are the contests held for the *sbandieratori* (standard bearers) and archers, which renew the ancient spirit of rivalry which existed between the Medieval cities. Attracted by the colorful parade, the imaginative choreography of the *sbandieratori* and the spirit of friendly rivalry typical of these manifestations, a numerous and enthusiastic public always attends to encourage and applaud their favorite team.

NEW SPACES AND NEW WALLS
FOR A GROWING CITY

The 'birth certificate' for the neighborhood of **Piano Scarano** (also spelled Scarlano or Squarano in the ancient chronicles) can be considered the document with which, in 1148, the friars of the monastery of Farfa sold the land where the *quartiere* is now located to the Magistrates of Viterbo. This area which the city had chosen for its expansion, during the period of domination by the Lombards had been used for drilling troops and the name of the site is probably derived from the Lombard word *squara*, a military detachment. In the 9th century documents record the existence here of a village called **Vico Squarano**. In any case when the Commune of Viterbo purchased the area from the Abbey of Farfa it was no longer inhabited. Construction of the first buildings in the new neighborhood began around the middle of the 12th century and the church dedicated to **San Andrea** must also have been built at this time. It was probably built where the old parish church of Vico Squarano had once stood, as Scriattoli maintains, citing the papal bull sent by Pope Leo IV in 852 to the Bishop of Toscanella (now called Tuscania) whose jurisdiction used to include the territory which later became the diocese of Viterbo, which mentions this church (in a passage, however, the meaning of which is not certain).

The church is prevalently Romanesque in style and has the raised presbytery typical of other churches in Viterbo. In the crypt there are stylistic elements which are apparently of a later period than those in the part that surmount it, like the cross-vaulted ceiling with ogival arches of the type usually found only in Cistercian Gothic. The church has been restored twice since the beginning of this century: the first time, in 1902 by order of Bishop Grasselli, who has already been mentioned in connection with the Church of San Pellegrino and who appointed as architect, the Viterbese Filippo Pincellotti; and the second time, immediately after the last war in order to repair the damage cause by the bombs.

Another monument of considerable interest in this quarter is the **fountain** located in the main square. This is a fine example of the spindle fountain which has already been mentioned, but it is famous for the most part because it is related to a dramatic event. In 1376 Pope Urban V was a guest in Viterbo and on his way back from Avignon had been housed in the fortress that the papal legate Cardinal Egidio Albornoz had had built just a few years earlier. Life in the city had become very animated due to the presence of numerous members of the retinue accompanying the pope on his trip and the relations between the citizens of Viterbo and their guests were not always totally friendly, mainly due to the proud and sometimes aggressive personality of the former and the conceited arrogance of the latter. In any case there was already a certain amount of tension in the air when some French servants who were part of the papal court insisted on washing a little dog in the fountain which provided drinking water for the people who lived in the neighborhood, and when these latter objected, refused to listen to their protests. The argument soon degenerated into a riot of major proportions as the inhabitants from other areas of the city came to the aid of their neighbors and Urban V's armed escort and dignitaries to the aid of the French. The situation of the pope's men soon became critical and, in the meantime, the Viterbese, made bold by their initial successes, were even proposing to assail the houses where the cardinals were staying. The Pope, frightened by what had turned into a major uprising, called out the militia from some of the nearby cities. The Viterbese suddenly realized that things had gone too far and tried to do something that would placate Urban V who was by that time threatening to have portions of the city walls and the towers knocked down, and to this purpose decided to demolish the houses of the leaders of the revolt as well as the fountain which had been the cause of the riot. The fountain was rebuilt many years later and this is the reason why it is the most recent of the city's spindle fountains. On the whole, the decoration of the central shaft (with lion heads framed by ogival arches supported by spiral columns) and the attractive cusp on top are more elegant than the earlier ones.

The great gate in the city walls which opens on to the quarter of Piano Scarano is called the **Porta del Carmine** after an ancient church which once stood on the spot and it is of particular interest because it the one which, not having been altered or remodeled in the past, has best maintained its original appearance. The reason for this is due to the fact that the gate, like the nearby gate of Porta San Pietro, did not mark the beginning of a particularly important road, and therefore in later years it was not deemed necessary to alter it in accordance with the new styles and tastes of the time in order to make it more worthy to welcome illustrious guests. The only other gates which were saved from this fate were the ones which for various reasons and in various eras were walled up.

Quarter of Piano Scarano,
the 12th century Church of San Andrea
probably built over the old
parish church of Vico Squarano.

The old gate of Porta di Valle closed in 1568 when the nearby gate of Porta Faul was built, and the remains of the apse of Santa Maria della Palomba. The road which connected the Via Cassia and the Cimina entered the city through this gate and left the city through the tower-gate of Porta S. Biele which had been built as an outpost outside the city walls.

Even today, if we except the two openings which represent a concession to the requirements of traffic and communication with the new suburban areas, the historic center of Viterbo is entirely encircled by walls. The **circle of walls** as it appears today was built when the gradual growth of the city had made the pre-existing defensive structures useless. These structures included natural obstacles like the ditch of Sonza, later called Urcionio, which surrounded the earlier village and which covered a triangle-shaped area which extended from the hill of the Cathedral to the old Porta Fiorita (remains of which can be seen at the Porta San Pietro) to the Porta Sonza, no longer extant, which was located at the point where the present day streets of Via Mazzini and Corso Italia intersect. As the city grew it became apparent that the newly inhabited areas would have to be included in some way within the defensive structure of the city, and this determined the construction of new walls which continued for over a century and a half. According to documents of the era, the first portion of walls was that between the gate of Porta Fiorita and Porta Sonza, built starting in 1095, and this included almost all of the part which today is flanked by the Cassia highway. After Piano Scarano had been purchased in the second half of the 12th century, the walls on the other side, from Porta Fiorita to the valley of Faul, beyond the hill of the cathedral, were built. A few years later, in 1208, building of the portion of walls which stopped at Ports Sonza was continued until it reached what is now the Piazza della Rocca; and in 1215 the walls were further extended until they reached the

Quarter of Piano Scarano, portion of the city walls.

*The Porta San Pietro gate and the Abbott's
Palace which once belonged to the
Carthusian Abbey of San Martino,
which became the property
of Lady Olimpia Pamphilj
in the middle of the 17th century.*

other side of the Valley of Faul. At this point the only part of the city left without walls was the narrow valley, considered less of a risk since the high cliffs on both sides made it easy to defend. This one remaining section however was soon closed in 1268 and the entire circle of walls was thus completed. The walls have been damaged several times due to wars and other causes and have always been repaired. The most recent and most dramatic event in which they have been involved was the last war, in which they were severely damaged by bombs and again had to be restored. However, in the past, restoration work was not so precise and complete as it is now. For example, it would appear that the walls that enclose the quarter of Piano Scarano now have fewer towers than they did originally because all of the towers had been torn down in the first half of the 13th century in accordance with a peace treaty with Rome after one of the many fights between the two cities, and were then rebuilt rapidly and in lesser quantity.

The gate of **Porta San Pietro** is located, as we have seen, in the oldest section of the city walls and replaced the nearby gate of Porta Fiorita and the citizens of Viterbo were often called to defend it from the attacks of the Roman militia. This gate was originally called the **Salicicchia** or **Salcicchia**, probably for the *selci* (flint stones) used for paving the access road and this name was soon transformed in **Salciccia**. The present day name is derived from that of a nearby church which, along with the convent attached to it, was founded around 1240 by cardinal Capocci as a Cistercian community and remodeled in the 17th century in the architectural style of that era.

Church of San Pietro, interior (below)
and façade (right).

The Palazzo which presides over the Porta San Pietro is also connected to the Cistercian order because it was built at the beginning of the 13th century by monks from the Abbey of San Martino al Cimino. It was intended as the residence for the leader of that community and for this reason was named **Palazzo dell'Abbate**, the Abbott's Palace; in 1654 it became the property of Donna Olimpia Maidalchini Pamphilj which she received from her brother-in-law, Pope Innocent X with the dominion of San Martino, along with the title of Princess. Among the various cardinals who, from the 14th to the 16th century, administered the Abbey when it was not being managed by the friars, one of the most significant was Francesco Todeschini Piccolomini, nephew of Pius II, who was later elected pope himself in 1503 with the name of Pius III. He had the palazzo consolidated and restored and among other things, had the elegant windows opened on the external side of the city walls. In 1568 the **Porta Faul** was opened in the walls; according to the inscription placed there it was called Farnesia in honor of Alessandro Farnese who was at that time papal legate in Viterbo, and the gate of the nearby Porta di Valle was closed as it was considered, according to the inscription, less suitable and convenient than the other. Outside the city walls, standing like a sentinel between the walls that join the Porta Romana to the Porta San Pietro, we find the **Portatorre di San Biele** which was built by the Capitano del Popolo, Raniero Gatti, who not only decorated it with the coat-of-arms of his family, but had an inscription attached which stated that it had been built without imposing any special taxes on the people of Viterbo. There are contrasting theories about the function of this gateway, through which the road leading from the city to the slopes of the Cimino passed. Some scholars believe that it was supposed to be an outpost of the fortified lines of the walls; others believe it was the beginning of a new circle of walls, conceived as an extra protection on a side which was more exposed than the others to enemy attacks. There are different opinions also on the origin of the name: the most probable of these is that proposed by Scriattoli which suggests that San Biele is a corruption of San Michele, to whom a nearby but no longer extant church was dedicated. The **Porta Vallia** gate, from which the above mentioned road left the city, was closed up around the middle of the 16th century. About a century later the nearby gate of Porta San Sisto was replaced by a wider and more decorative one which was called the **Porta Romana**. It had originally been made for the visit of Pope Innocent X to Viterbo in 1653 and in 1705 was remodeled to the appearance which we see today. It is decorated with the coats-of-arms of Popes Innocent X and Clement XI and a statue of St. Rose of Viterbo on top; the dents made by the cannonballs shot by the French in 1798 to overcome the resistance of the Viterbese are still visible.

The **Monastery of Santa Maria in Gradi** is located at the beginning of the street which goes from the gate toward Ronciglione. This complex was built by order of Cardinal Raniero Capocci for a Dominican community and the original church was replaced in the 18th century by another designed by Nicola Salvi who was the architect of the Trevi Fountain in Rome. It was irreparably damaged in the last war and the only part of the structure which still maintains the original features (though it was built a few decades later) is the cloister, which was built in the second half of the 13th century. The

Porta Romana.

Porta Romana, the statue of Santa Rosa and the coats-of-arms of Popes Innocent X and Clement XI at the top of the gate.

Church of San Sisto, façade (above)
and the ancient Lombard bell-tower
with a little column
shaped like a person (right).

Church of San Sisto, interior.

monastery was expropriated after Viterbo became part of unified
Italy and was used as a penitentiary which was transformed only
recently into a modern prison. It then changed hands, passing from
the Prison Administration to the University of Tuscia, and is now
about to be restored again in order to repair the damage caused by
bombing in the last war and the alterations necessary for the removal
of the prison structures.

Near to the Porta Romana is the **Church of San Sisto** which is built
up against the city walls and whose apse projects beyond the walls.
This church is one of the oldest and most interesting in the city. It
was built over the ruins of the ancient parish church of Vico Quin-
zano (one of the tiny villages later absorbed into the urban area of
Viterbo). It was probably built in the 11th century, though some
scholars maintain that it may even have been built in the 9th. It was
enlarged during the following two centuries with the construction of
the raised presbytery and the apse, which required cutting through
the walls. The oldest parts of the church are the little bell-tower
with its typical Lombard architectural elements, like the tiny arches
and the capitals of the triple windows which are similar to those of
Santa Maria della Cella and the Cloister of Santa Maria Nuova, and
the three naves. When the church was enlarged in the 13th century
a larger bell-tower was added. For this purpose one of the towers of
the city gates was used and the bell room was built on top of it. To
the right of the main altar the visitor can admire a beautiful painting of the *Madonna and Child among Angels and Saints* attributed
to Neri di Bicci (first half of the 15th century). The church was
severely damaged during the last war and has only recently been
restored.

FROM PORTA ROMANA TO PORTA DELLA VERITÀ
WALKING ALONG
THE STREETS OF THE DOWNTOWN

The layout of the streets of the historic center of Viterbo was profoundly modified between the second half of the 16th century and the end of the 17th. Before that time the main thoroughfare crossing Viterbo was the one that led from the Cimini going towards Porta S. Biele and Porta S. Leonardo, ran close by Piazza San Silvestro, reached the hill of the Cathedral and then descended until it intersected with the old portion of the Via Cassia. This roadway clearly had been designed with the old village center in mind, but it had become peripherical since the center of the administrative and political activity of the city had been moved to Piazza del Plebiscito. The importance of moving the access roads towards this square was brought up in 1573 by Cardinal Alessandro Farnese who then held the title of perpetual legate in the city. He decided to build a new road which would connect in a straight line the plaza which contained the municipal office buildings with the Plaza of the Fontana Grande (great fountain), and he levied a tax of "one *grosso* for every bushel of grain that was ground into flour" (thus establishing a precedent for the infamous flour tax levied during the first years of the United Kingdom of Italy) in order to pay the compensation due to the owners of the houses which had to be torn down to make way for it. Toward the end of the 16th century the new street was completed and the coats-of-arms which decorate the two extremities recall the two popes who were in office while work was going on: Pope Gregory XIII and Sixtus V. Officially the street was named Farnesina, but by the people it was always called the **Via Nuova** (new street); in 1814 the name was changed for a brief time to Via Napoleone, and then in 1870 its name was changed to **Via Cavour**, which is what it is called today.

About a century after the construction of this road, Michelangelo de' Conti who was then governor of Viterbo (and was later elected pope with the name of Innocent XIII) decided to continue the work begun by Cardinal Farnese by building a new street to connect the Piazza Fontana Grande to the gate of Porta Romana, thus completing the access road leading directly from the civic center to the city walls in 1695. The street was named after him until, after the unification of Italy, it was dedicated to Giuseppe Garibaldi.

The **Great Fountain**, therefore, is located about half-way along this street which is still one of the most important streets leading to the civic center. Of the many fountains that embellish the squares of Viterbo, it is certainly the most original and harmoniously combines elements from many different styles, including most of the main architectural details of the Middle Ages but it cannot be classified in any specific stylistic category. The ancient chronicles say that it was built starting in 1206 and an inscription states that it was completed only in 1279. A century and a half later, in 1424 it was restored. It was originally called *Fons Sepalis*, a name which appears to have derived from a hedge (*siepe*) which grew around the area and where another earlier fountain had stood. This name soon was transformed into "Separi" which, in honor of its beauty soon became *"sine pari"*, i.e. without equal. The fountain was always held in particular consideration and the City Statutes specifically stated that anyone who removed the drain plug from the basin or sullied its waters would be fined.

The Great Fountain with the 17th century church of the Carmelitani Scalzi in the background.

The **Church of the Carmelitani Scalzi** with its 17th century façade is located at the far end of the square and together with the convent next to it was expropriated in 1876 for use as judiciary offices. The court of Assizes was set up in the church and several famous trials have been held here, like the Cuocolo trial during the first decade of this century and, during the 1950s the trial against Salvatore Giuliano and his band. This complex stands on the area which was previously occupied by the Palazzo of the Gatti family, which was almost totally destroyed by the Viterbese, instigated by Pope Alexander VI at the end of the 15th century. A wing of the Palazzo, recently restored, still exists on the Via Cardinal La Fontaine nearby. The shape of the biforus windows presents evident analogies with those used in the Papal Palace, which is thought to have been built in the same era.

As we walk along Via Cavour going towards the Piazza del Plebiscito, it is worth stopping to admire, on the right at the top of a stairway, an interesting example of a 14th century house, **Casa Poscia**, named after one of the families that lived there. Scholars have tried to interpret what remains of a ruined coat-of-arms, and the house has been attributed to various families that had important roles in Viterbo's history in the Late Middle Ages, and even to Galiana, the beautiful young woman made famous by the legend which we have mentioned earlier.

From the Piazza del Plebiscito another thoroughfare, consisting of Via Roma and Corsa Italia, crosses through what is now the civic center and reaches the place where the gate of Porta Sonza once stood. Between the two streets we find the **Piazza delle Erbe** (the Plaza of

*Façade of the Church
of the Carmelitani Scalzi.*

*Piazza delle Erbe with
its 17th century fountain.*

the Herbs) which has an elegant fountain in the center designed by the
Viterbese painter Filippo Caparozzi and built in 1621. When the fountain was restored in 1877 another Viterbese artist, the sculptor Pio
Fedi, donated the four marble lions which were used to replace the
original ones. There were once important buildings near the piazza, like
the Church dedicated to Saint Stephen and a Palazzo which belonged
to the Gatti family, but nothing of these remain except a few coats-of-
arms and other minor relics. Worthy of note is the handsome building
at the corner of the Corso which is called the **Casa della Pace** (House
of Peace) because it bears an inscription which recalls one of the many
attempts to put an end to civil strife (1503). Along the **Corso Italia**
(which is the traditional strolling place in Viterbo) we find among other
interesting sites, two churches which were built by ancient confraterni-
ties. The first of these was erected by the Confraternita del Suffragio
and is named after it; the second, which has a handsome polygonal
apse that can be admired from Via Marconi, was dedicated to San
Egidio and is now deconsecrated.

If the Corso Italia has been rightly defined as the parlor of the city, then
the most intimate and elegant corner of this parlor is without a doubt
the **Caffè Schenardi**, which within the obvious limitations imposed by

Piazza Alighieri with its spindle fountain and the side of the Church of San Giovanni in Zoccoli in the background.

Piazza Alighieri, detail of the spindle fountain.

the modest environment of a provincial city, carries on the cultural and social tradition of the most famous Italian Caffès. The Caffè was founded in 1818 when a Neapolitan, Raffaele Schenardi, bought the rooms in the building in which the Chigi family had opened a bank in the 16th century, and which two centuries later had been turned into a hotel. The name of Albergo Reale (Royal Inn) was appropriate, as Queen Christina of Sweden and Ferdinand IV of the Two Sicilies and his wife had stayed there. The architect Vespignani (better known for having built the Teatro Comunale dell'Unione) was appointed to design the hall, which after being carefully restored several years ago, still retains the severe lines of the original plan, with a double set of cross-vaulted ceilings supported by slender columns. Besides the usual gossip and political discussions, many important cultural initiatives have taken shape and been promoted in these rooms, where for many decades one of the owners, recently deceased, Renzo Javarone, fought tirelessly for the protection and appreciation of the natural wonders and the art treasures of Viterbo and its environs.

Towards the end of the Corso, on the right, is **Via Mazzini** which starts in about the same spot where the gate of Porta Sonza opened through the city walls. An inscription on a stone plaque attached to the building at the corner of the two streets reminds us that this gate enjoyed a privileged status; in fact, the Emperor Henry IV of Swabia decreed that any citizen of Viterbo that passed through the Porta Sonza would be freed from all bonds of servitude. Continuing along Via Mazzini the visitor should take note of the many interesting monuments of the past: two beautiful spindle fountains, the Church of Santa Maria in Poggio (also called Santa Maria della Crocetta) where the body of Saint Rosa of Viterbo was placed right after her death, but which was remodeled in the 17th century; the Renaissance Palazzo of the Nini family, which recalls the first marriage of Lady Olimpia Maidalchini, who, upon her second marriage, became the sister-in-law of Pope Innocent X; and the Church of Santa Caterina where Vittoria Colonna stayed and which is now surrounded by school buildings. Of particular interest is also the **Church of San Giovanni in Zoccoli**, which still retains the austere simplicity of the Romanesque style. In the severe and unembellished forms of this church Scriattoli saw the influence of Paleo-Christian art and suggested that the name of the church, which originally was spelled *San Giovanni in Ciocola*, comes from the word *ciotola* (the little bowl) which the Saint used to baptize the faithful.

San Giovanni is one of the oldest churches in the city and is believed to have been built in the first half of the 11th century, a date which is in part based on a statement by the 17th century historian, Feliciano Bussi, who said that he had seen the date 1037 etched on one of the bells of the church before it was removed to be melted down. The interior, with three naves, has a structure which is analogous to that of the other Romanesque churches of the city, except perhaps for the fact that its general appearance is even more austere, in part due to the simple torus-shaped capitals which have none of the decorations found on those of the Cathedral and Santa Maria Nuova. The capitals are surmounted by round arches and supported by simple straight columns. Of particular interest is also the elegant rose-window of the façade with *symbols of the Four Evangelists* and a beautiful Cosmatesque decoration datable to some time after the 12th century Among other important works that are kept in this church, the *Episcopal throne* carved in

*Façade of the Church
of San Giovanni in Zoccoli.*

*Interior of the Church
of San Giovanni in Zoccoli.*

*San Giovanni in Zoccoli, interior, detail
of the poliptych by Francesco d'Antonio,
called Il Balletta.*

stone located in the central apse and the poliptych of 1441 which represents the *Madonna enthroned with various Saints* by the Viterbese painter Francesco d'Antonio, called Il Balletta, are particularly noteworthy.

At the end of Via Mazzini there is a short street which is named after a 15th Viterbese historian, Niccolò della Tuccia, whose house was nearby. This street leads to the **Porta della Verità**, a 13th century gate which was restored and enlarged in 1728 in honor of the visit that Pope Benedict XIII had paid to the city the year before. The coat-of-arms of the pope, along with that of the governor, Oddi, the Bishop, Sermattei, and the Commune of Viterbo are visible on the outside walls. Inside, an inscription on a stone plaque informs us that on October 24th 1867, a group of Garibaldi's men who were part of a division being led by General Acerbi, tried in vain to enter the city and, in the fight which ensued, two of them were killed along with a friar from the nearby Convent of the Servites.

Porta della Verità.

MEMORIES OF ANCIENT TUSCIA WITHIN THE PREMONSTRATENSE WALLS

The Porta della Verità (Gate of the Truth) also once known as the Gate of Saint Matthew or the Gate of the Abbott, is, by all three of these names connected to the Monastery standing outside of it, just a few yards from the city walls. The monastic complex was founded in the second half of the 12th century by a community of monks of the Premonstratense order. This order was founded in the French valley of Prémontré in 1120 by a nobleman from Lorraine, Saint Norbert. About a century later the monastery was taken over by friars of the Servite order from Monte Senario who remained there until, after the unification of Italy, the church and the convent were expropriated by the State in accordance with the laws relating to the secularization of the ecclesiastical property. For many years the monastery buildings were used as a school and the church was used for the Civic Museum which was opened in 1912. The complex was severely damaged by bombing in the last war, was restored under the auspices of the Superintendency of Monuments and reopened as a church.

The **church** is thought to be contemporary with the earliest structures of the monastery. It presents many elements which are typical of Cistercian architecture, and are here even more evident than in many other buildings in the area, like the famous abbeys of Santa Maria di Falleri and San Martino al Cimino, which are considered typical examples of this style. The elegant cloister was built about two centuries later and its refined lines are indicative of a much more advanced stage in the interpretation of the elements typical of French Gothic architecture.

Though the original structure was built in the 12th century, it was during the 15th century, according to Scriattoli, "that the modest Premonstratense church was transformed into the majestic temple which had ignited such fervid Christian piety in the city". The numerous chapels and altars commissioned by the leading families of Viterbo and lavishly decorated with paintings by the most famous artists of the day and the tombs commissioned by the professional guilds amply demonstrate the truth of this statement. Scriattoli, a local historian, added that the church was so greatly venerated "that it was considered an honor to be buried therein".

Without a doubt the most precious 'jewel' in the church of Santa Maria della Verità, is the **Mazzatosta Chapel** which was decorated with frescoes in 1469 by a young artist, Lorenzo of Viterbo, whose premature death prevented him from becoming one of the great painters of his era. Among the paintings which decorate the Chapel, of particular interest is the beautiful fresco on the left wall with the *Marriage of the Virgin*, in which the painter has given life to the various figures which occupy the scene in a particularly lively and natural manner. The fresco is also interesting as a faithful reconstruction of typical costumes of the 15th century (era to which the scene is referred, as was usual at the time). In this painting we can also admire the face of Lorenzo himself, as his self-portrait appears on the left as the figure who is talking to Nardo Mazzatosta (the man who had had the Chapel built a few years earlier and commissioned the frescoes), the portrait of the city historian Niccolò della Tuccia (the information contained in his Chronicles not only tell us that his

Santa Maria della Verità. Interior.

*Santa Maria della Verità, Mazzatosta
Chapel, detail of the
Marriage of the Virgin,
fresco by Lorenzo da Viterbo.*

Opposite page: *Santa Maria della Verità.
Mazzatosta Chapel.*

*Santa Maria della Verità, left transept,
Madonna with Child and Saints,
fresco of the 14th century,School
of Viterbo* (right) *and detail of the
ceiling of the Mazzatosta Chapel* (below).

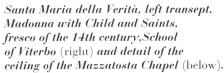

portrait was painted on April 26th 1469, but also give us the details
necessary for locating it), and many other well known figures of 15th
century Viterbo. Notwithstanding the fact that the church was almost
totally destroyed by bombs in the last war, we can still enjoy the
beauty of this wonderful work of art thanks to the almost miraculous
restoration made by the Central Restoration Institute. It is interesting
to note that the team that restored the painting was greatly assisted
in their work by the existence of a faithful copy of the fresco made by
the Viterbese painter Pietro Vanni in 1889, which is kept in the Sala
Rossa (Red Hall) of the Palazzo dei Priori.
The convent which is located next to the church has been the **Civic
Museum** since 1955. Italo Faldi, a scholar who did research on the

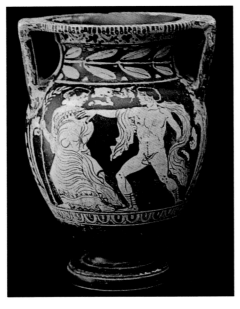

origins of the Museum collections, recalls the interest aroused in the second half of the 15th century by the Dominican friar Giovanni Annio, who became famous not only for his doctrine but also (and perhaps mainly) for the impudence with which he 'created' documents and traditions to an extent which muddied the waters of research on the history of Viterbo for decades and even for centuries. In any case it was mostly due to interest aroused by his studies that some Etruscan sarcophaguses found in the nearby necropolis were placed in the Palazzo Comunale and this was the starting point of the collection which during the three centuries which followed was enlarged and enriched by additions and donations. The objects in the collection were first catalogued scientifically between 1816 and 1821 by the Accademia degli Ardenti of Viterbo acting on a proposal by one of their members, Stefano Camilli; in 1848 the Etruscan section was authoritatively catalogued by the great English archeologist George Dennis. Around the middle of the century however a lack of interest towards the collections is apparent on the part of the Accademia, and part of the collection was lost.

The problem of creating a museum arose again after 1870, in part because it was obvious that something had to be done about the art work from the churches and convents which had been suppressed in accordance with the law which has been previously mentioned, relating to the secularization of ecclesiastical property. At first the material was arranged on the ground floor of the Palazzo Comunale; it was later transferred, in 1912, to the Church of Santa Maria della Verità. When this church, as previously mentioned, was rebuilt after the last war, the collection was moved to its present location.

The Museum is divided into two sections. The first section is displayed on the ground floor in the corridors of the cloister and the adjacent rooms and consists of the archeological collections which include artifacts from the Etruscan and Roman periods, with numerous objects from tombs, sarcophaguses, sculpture, and other material. The other section of the Museum is located on the second story and includes paintings, sculpture and other works of art from the Middle Ages to the 18th century. Of particular interest, especially in relation to local history, is the collection of sketches of various models for the "machine" of Santa Rosa, different versions of which have been used for over three centuries for the annual procession which takes place on the evening of September 3rd. This is a manifestation which expresses a profound devotion of the people to the Saint; it will be described in detail in the next chapter.

Civic Museum of Viterbo, archeological section, artifacts of the Etrusco-Roman period (top and center). *Picture Gallery, Pietà by Sebastiano del Piombo* (left).

THE FASCINATING MAGIC OF THE "MOVING BELL-TOWER" AS THE LEGEND OF SANTA ROSA IS RE-ENACTED EVERY YEAR

The area of the city which is encompassed by Via Mazzini, Piazza Verdi and the city walls is connected more than any other with the legend of Santa Rosa, a young girl who lived in the first half of the 13th century and who was sanctified by popular demand before papal authority or the usual procedure for canonization had officially declared her a Saint. She was probably born in 1233 to a poor family and was venerated even as a very young child for, according to tradition, at only three years of age she resuscitated an aunt on her deathbed. Rosa dedicated her brief life (she is generally thought to have died in 1251) to prayer, the mortification of the flesh, and comforting the poor and the afflicted. According to the legend, during the struggle of the Guelph party of Viterbo against the emperor Frederick II, the simple words of a common girl convinced the citizens of Viterbo to unite in their fight and resist the attack of the Imperial troops. Her ability to inspire and animate the people caused her to be sent in to exile with her family and, in the dead of winter they were forced to leave Viterbo and cross over the mountains of Cimini, covered with snow, to reach the village of Soriano. It was at this time that Rosa is supposed to have prophesied the death of Frederick II, an event which soon determined a major change in political events, the end of her exile, and her return to Viterbo.

A few years before her death Rosa had already begun to wear the habit of a member of the Third Order of Franciscans. She had also asked in vain of the Mother Superior of the Convent of San Damiano near her home, to be admitted as one of the nuns of St. Clare. Her wish was finally granted in 1258 when her body was found totally intact in the Church of Santa Maria del Poggio where it had been buried in the raw earth, and was carried in triumph to the convent by four cardinals while the pope himself, Alexander IV, led the pious procession. The hearing for her canonization was initiated immediately but was never terminated, nevertheless, starting in this year the cult of Santa Rosa (encouraged by the presence of the pope at her funeral) spread rapidly and in 1512 was officially approved with the creation of an annual manifestation with a procession which re-evoked the removal of her body to the convent. Since the beginning of the 14th century the church of **Santa Maria delle Rose** and the adjacent convent of San Damiano have frequently been called with the name of Santa Rosa.

At a certain point therefore it was deemed necessary to embellish the humble little church of the Sisters of San Damiano in order to make it worthy of the honor derived from the presence of the body of the Saint, who in the meantime had been named patron saint of the city along with St. Lawrence. This is the reason why so much remodeling and enlarging began to take place and continued for centuries: starting with the *Stories from the Life of Santa Rosa* painted in 1453 by Benozzo Gozzoli in a series of frescoes which were unfortunately destroyed during alterations made in 1632, followed by the complete reconstruction of the church after the demolition of the pre-existing one around the middle of the 19th century by order of Cardinal Gaspare Bernardo Pianetti, then Bishop of Viterbo, and finally, the present day structure completed in the first decades of this century by the architect Arnaldo Foschini who designed the cupola which has now become one of the most characteristic features of the city skyline. Other changes were made in the interior of the church during the 1930s. Among the major art works which are still kept in Santa Rosa, the visitor can admire, on the second altar on the left, an elaborate triptych painted in 1441 by Francesco d'Antonio, called Il Balletta, which depicts the *Madonna enthroned with Santa Rosa and Saint Catherine of Alexandria*, and other saints represented in the smaller spaces. Another object of great devotion, in a chapel on the right closed by a metal screen, is the *perfectly preserved body of the Saint* which is enclosed in a sumptuous urn commissioned in 1683 by Cardinal Urbano Sacchetti who was elected Bishop of the city in that year. In a narrow side street which runs next to the monastery there is the house where, according to the inscription on it, "Santa Rosa was born, lived and died". In the past the little house had been incorporated into the convent structures. It was restored in 1936 and, with its simple impoverished appearance, is a very touching sight for visitors.

Church of Santa Rosa, interior.

Church of Santa Rosa, poliptych by Francesco d'Antonio called Il Balletta (left), *dome designed by Foschini (1915) and detail of one of the four Evangelists* (above).

The memory of this youthful Saint however is perpetuated not so much by Foschini's majestic dome as by the unique manifestation held in her honor every September 3rd in the evening: this event consists of a funeral procession in which the "machine" dedicated to Santa Rosa, a tower structure almost one hundred feet tall, is carried on the shoulders of hundreds of strong young men of Viterbo, along the streets of the historic downtown for about a half a mile. The "machine" sparkles with the lights that decorate it, the public admires and applauds it, the common people are touched as this annual spectacle is repeated every year and marks the sad and happy moments of an entire existence, and the tourists look on with astonished curiosity because the manifestation is invariably better than it has been represented or described.

According to tradition this pious and spectacular act of devotion is carried out in fulfillment of a vow which was made by the citizens of Viterbo during the terrible plague of 1657; but as a procession already seems to have existed in 1512, and was probably only the official recognition of a cult that already had many adherents, and documents exist describing a "machine" in 1654, this would tend to indicate that some kind of manifestation was being held long before that time, and that it must be interpreted as a re-evocation of the moving of the body of Santa Rosa in 1258 initiated by and in the presence of Pope Alexander IV.

In the beginning it was probably just a procession in which a statue of the Saint was carried. The oldest drawings of machines are from the second half of the 17th century, and therefore were made in the years immediately following the plague which some scholars believe gave rise to the tradition. These drawings show structures of a modest height in which the statue is enclosed in a kind of tabernacle supported by a low base. The earliest "machines" therefore were made up of these two elements. In later machines we can observe that the two elements became ever more widely separated as other structures were inserted between them, and this may be considered the first sign of the tendency to become higher, which after an initial development using the Neo-Classical forms typical of the beginning of the 19th century, began to tend more and more toward Gothic lines, as this was apparently the most suitable style for a slender vertical structure which was supposed to look as though it were reaching toward heaven. The aforementioned collection of drawings representing various models of "machines" from the 17th century until the present, is housed in the Civic Museum and, though the series is not complete, it still gives a good idea of how the "machines" evolved from a simple simulacrum to an immense "moving bell-tower."

The collection of drawings includes not only the shapes of the various "machines" but also the names of the builders like Franceschini, Tacchini, Bordoni, Spadini and a true dynasty of builders, the Papini family who, except for a few brief intervals continued to invent and construct models, some of which were true works of art, for over 130 years (1820-1951). Angelo and his wife Rosa, then Raffaele, Pier Felice, Paolo e Virgilio Papini, all dedicated their lives to the exaltation of the Saint of Viterbo, with a demonstration of faith which remained unchanged throughout periods of profound political and social unrest, from the last fifty years of existence of the Papal State through the turmoil of two world wars. After the death of Virgilio Papini, who succeeded his father Paolo and continued to design "machines" for over fifty years, Rodolfo Salcini was appointed to design and build them. His model, which was built by Romano Giusti, was carried from 1952 until 1958. The model of Angelo Paccosi was carried from 1959 until 1966 and represented a return to tradition; Giuseppe Zucchi (1967-78) created a particularly original model which was called "Angel's Flight" in place of the old name of the "Moving Bell-tower". The designers of the most recent "machines" are, in chronological order, Antonietta Palazzetti Valeri (1979-85), another woman designer after Rosa Papini in the mid 1800s, Roberto Joppolo (1986-90) and the present designer, Angelo Russo. Their creations have often received imaginative names: Spiral of Faith, Celestial Harmony, and Symphony of Violins. For the past few years, the procession which carries the heart of the Saint, takes place on the afternoon of September 2nd and is proceeded by groups dressed in historic costumes: the city magistrates of the 13th-18th century accompanied by their dignitaries. The procession is organized by the nuns of the order of St. Clare who are the custodians of the Sanctuary which contains the remains of the Patron Saint, and these same nuns are responsible for the beautiful costumes.

The external framework of the "machine", modeled in wood and papier- maché used to be supported by huge, heavy wooden beams; several decades ago these were replaced by a frame of metal screen.

The new machine of Santa Rosa
'The start of the third millenium - a Rose for the year 2000'.

The whole structure weighs thousands of pounds: the most recent ones have weighed five metric tons. The men that carry the tower are traditionally called *facchini* (porters) and in recent years have been officially honored with the title of "Cavaliere di Santa Rosa". They wear a special white costume with a red band around the waist and a white handkerchief knotted on their heads. The porters who have participated in the procession for at least ten years have the right to wear a blue band at the waist instead of the red one. A pad is used to protect the shoulders of the porters on the sides who are called *"spallette"*. The porters who walk in the compact rows lined up directly beneath the base of the *macchina*, and are therefore the ones which must support the greatest amount of weight, have their head and shoulders protected by a stiff leather cap called a *"ciuffo"* and these porters are called with this name. For these men there is a complicated tradition involving a precise ritual which must be observed relating to the costume, a period of 'seclusion' followed by visits to some of the churches in the hours directly preceding the procession, and then a benediction given *in articulo mortis*, like soldiers leaving for a war.

Actually the history of the procession includes several episodes which confirm the real danger present in the transport of the *macchina*. In 1801 the panic created by the screams of a woman who had just been robbed caused such a precipitous flight that twenty-two spectators were killed, trampled to death in the confusion. Thirteen years later, two porters were killed and two were wounded when the huge structure fell over during the *mossa*, i.e. the difficult starting maneuvers. Fortunately only one person was wounded in 1820 when Angelo Papini's *macchina* was first used. It fell as it was being carried along the

Designs for 'machines' of Santa Rosa of the 19th century.

Union Theatre, façade.

Corso after swaying violently due to the fact, according to the story, that most of the porters were drunk after having at length celebrated the creation of the new model. More recently, in 1893 a torrential rainstorm which had prevented the procession from taking place, averted a terrorist attack on the part of a group of anarchists who were going to use explosive bottles (an early version of the Molotov cocktail). In 1967 the group carrying Zucchi's first *macchina* swerved widely and though no one was hurt the procession had to be called off.

It is worthwhile mentioning also some of the important persons who, in different eras, have attended the procession of the *macchina* of Santa Rosa. Among them are several popes of the past: Pius VII, Gregory XVI, Pius IX: in our era, king Gustaf VI Adolph of Sweden who, due to his interest in Etruscology was particularly fond of Viterbo and of the Tuscia region where he had conducted a number of important archeological excavations in various parts of the province; and, most recently, Pope John Paul II who on May 27th 1984, at the end of a day spent in Viterbo watched from a window of the Palazzo dei Priori an 'extraordinary' procession, extraordinary not only because it took place on a date that was different from the usual one, but because a furious rainstorm was going on which made carrying the *macchina* particularly difficult.

The **Teatro Unione** (Union Theatre) was designed by the architect, Virginio Vespignani, who was also responsible for the remodeling of the Caffe Schenardi, mentioned above. The building of the theatre was initiated by a group of private citizens and took place from 1846 to 1855: it is now the property of the city of Viterbo. The building, with its austere and elegant Neo-Classical architecture is connected in various ways to many of the most important events in the recent history of the city, starting with the patriotic demonstrations during the struggle for Italian unification (the *Risorgimento*) to the dramatic bombing attacks of the last war, in which the building was severely damaged. After the war the theatre was restored and since then it has been partially remodeled several times. It is worth mentioning that during the Opera seasons of the past, the Teatro Unione has seen the debut of some of the most prestigious singing voices of our time, among these, Giacomo Lauri Volpi.

The façade of the theatre closes the far end of Piazza Giuseppe Verdi, like the curtain on a stage. On the side of this plaza are located the ancient church of San Marco and the 15th century Palazzo Santoro.

An inscription tells us that the church was consecrated on December 1st 1198 by Pope Innocent III in the presence of fifteen cardinals. This last detail prompted the Viterbese historian Andrea Scriattoli to inquire jokingly how they had possibly all managed to fit inside: in fact, the church is so tiny and narrow that this is a good question. Inside the little church is very simple and unadorned except for a 16th century painting on a wooden panel which is attributed to a local painter, Giovan Francesco d'Avanzarano, called *Il Fantastico*.

On the other side of the plaza is the Palazzo that Cardinal Nicola Fortiguerra, papal legate in Viterbo (and therefore resident of the city) and Captain of the papal militia, had built in 1466. The Palazzo, which now houses the Biblioteca Comunale (Municipal library) and the adjacent archives, is known by the name of its second owner, Cardinal Fazio Santoro. The building, like many others here, was severely damaged in the last war and rebuilt after the war.

ANCIENT LEGENDS
AND THE REMEMBRANCE OF THINGS PAST
IN THE CHURCH OF SAN FRANCESCO
AND THE CHURCH OF THE TRINITY

The northern portion of the city walls is dominated by the great bulk of the Rocca or fortress, built by order of Cardinal Egidio Albornoz in 1354. During this period the popes had already been in Avignon for several decades and their absence had determined a progressive weakening of their power in the territories of the State of the Church, which were increasingly abandoned to the influence of local despots. In this critical situation, it was thought that the presence of this powerful Spanish cardinal might be the best way to restore order in the papal dominions, and in fact, one of Albornoz's first acts was to build a fortress that would enable him to maintain military control over the cities which were politically the most important and the least secure. This was the reason why the Rocca was built in Viterbo, though the building as we see it now, is still being restored after the damage suffered in the last war, and is completely different from the way Albornoz had conceived it. The cardinal in fact was not able to finish the construction and on several occasions the inhabitants of Viterbo had actually attacked this symbol of papal power, causing damage and devastation. Finally, various popes became involved in the building of the Rocca in order to modify it and suit it to the altered tastes and different requirements of the time. In this way the

La Rocca, and the plaza of the same name. On the front of the fortress is the loggia which Pope Paul III had built in the 16th century.

*Piazza della Rocca with its fountain
designed by Vignola.*

*Piazza della Rocca, in the background
the building which was formerly
the Hotel Grandori named after
its founder who wanted Viterbo
to have first class hotels (1888).*

fortress gradually lost the austere appearance of a defensive structure and acquired a softer and more elegant form.

This transformation became complete when Pope Paul III had a great loggia opened in the building in the first half of the 16th century. Under his predecessor Clement VII, the Knights Hospitaller of St. John of Jerusalem had stayed briefly at the Rocca, after having been forced to leave Rhodes by the advancing Turkish armies; after leaving Viterbo they settled on the Island of Malta, from which they took the name with which they were later known.

In the plaza in front of the Rocca there is a great fountain, which, with its typical Renaissance style, appears totally different from most of the other fountains of Viterbo all of which have Medieval features. The fountain, in fact was designed by Vignola, who was at the time engaged in the construction of the lavish Palazzo that Cardinal Alessandro Farnese, nephew of Pope Paul III, was building in Caprarola. It was built under the direction of a Viterbese, Paolo Cenni in 1566, but it soon became apparent that the construction was not stable due principally to the excessive weight of the elements at the top, and since it was considered dangerous, was dismantled shortly afterward. However, the various parts of the fountain were reused at the end of the century by the Roman architect, Giovanni Malanca, who was able to eliminate all the original structural defects and rebuild it.

On the east side of the plaza there is a brief slope that leads to the **Church of San Francesco.** It is built on the top of a hill which, in the Lombard period, was occupied by a fortress called the Castle of Sonza; when the Canons of the Church of Saint Angelo acquired the zone in the 11th century, the church was named after the fortress. In 1208 the castle was torn down and in its place was erected a Palazzo which was called "degli Alemanni" where popes and emperors stayed for almost three centuries when they visited Viterbo.

The Church of San Francesco and the adjacent convent were built on lands that were donated to the Franciscans by Pope Gregory IX in 1236. The building was modified and rebuilt many times over a period of several centuries, in particular it was remodeled at the expense of the wealthy Botonti family in 1603. The church was totally destroyed during a bomb attack on January 17th 1944 which left only portions of the external walls standing. It was completely restored to its original appearance after the war. For example, when the main doorway (which had been completely destroyed) was

San Francesco,
Romanesque doorway of the façade.

Façade of San Francesco (left);
pulpit located at the right corner
of the façade, from which San Bernardino
of Siena preached
to the people of Viterbo in 1426 (below).

San Francesco, interior.

rebuilt the little spiral columns which had been used in the original doorway of 1372 and replaced with others in 1465 were reused. These little columns had been discovered after the bombing, inserted in the left side of the church. San Bernardino of Siena preached to the populace of Viterbo from the pulpit which is located on the right side of the façade.

Inside the church with its single nave, the roof has been rebuilt in its original form *a capriate*, supported by a truss and beam structure, while the transepts and the presbyterium have the cross vaulted ceilings typical of Cistercian architecture.

There were once numerous important tombs in this church, portions of which still remain after the bombing. The two most important, located at the sides of the presbyterium have been completely restored: the tombs of Pope Clement IV and Adrian V who died in Viterbo in 1268 and in 1276. These are two magnificent sepulchral monuments which for their unique architectural and decorative elements can be considered true masterpieces. The first of these tombs was originally placed in the church of Santa Maria in Gradi (where Clement wished to be buried) and later was involved in a long series of vicissitudes because the Canons of the Cathedral immediately insisted on having the honor of having the pope buried in their church and had the tomb moved. The monument along with the body of the pope was returned to its original site only when Pope Gregory X threatened them with excommunication. At the end of the 18th century during the period of the Republic of Rome, the tomb was tampered with: finally in 1870 when the church of Santa Maria in Gradi was expropriated by the Italian government, the tomb was transferred to San Francesco. The monument is attributed to Pietro d'Oderisio. The tomb of Adrian V, in which Cosmatesque type mosaics are inserted into an essentially Gothic structure, has been variously attributed to Arnolfo di Cambio and Vassalletto.

Next to the Rocca of Albornoz, along the city walls, in 1480 Pope Sixtus IV had a great building constructed as a stable, and this was commonly called *lo stallone del Papa* (the Pope's big stalls). The buildings were later used as a prison and called "Sallupara", then as barracks which were almost totally destroyed during the last war and are now abandoned ruins. Nearby we find the little **plaza of San Faustino**, which is at the center of a neighborhood which, according to the ancient chronicles, started to be built up after the destruction of the city of Ferento in 1172. The area was included within the circle of city walls in 1210. In the middle of the plaza there is a spindle fountain which we know was built in 1251 because it is mentioned in a statute emanated that year. The main shaft of the fountain bears the name of the builders: Giacomo d'Andrea and Gemini di Maestro Francesco. Of particular interest are the coats-of-arms carved in relief on the cusp.

The architecture of the **Church of San Faustino and Giovita,** as it appears today, has no relation whatever with the original structure which was probably contemporary with the fountain, because it was radically rebuilt around the middle of the 18th century and restored in 1911. For this reason the building is important chiefly for the works of art which is contains, like the *Virgin of Constantinopoli,* a Byzantine image of the Madonna which reminds us that the Knights Hospitaller of St. John of Jerusalem used this church for their rites

during their stay in Viterbo. There are also two paintings attributed to the 18th Viterbese painter Vincenzo Strigelli.

The Sanctuary of **Maria SS. Liberatrice or della Trinità** is located where, in the first half of the 13th century, there once stood a humble little church, at that time outside of the village, which is mentioned in a document dated 1237. The city walls terminated in fact before they reached the plaza which is now dominated by the façade of the Sanctuary, and at the point where the street coming from Piazza San Faustino ends there was a gate which was called the *Porticella*. According to an inscription there, this gate was torn down "in order to widen the road and make the place healthier" because "its great height prevented the evil winds from being blown away". According to one of Friar Annio's fanciful pieces of information, the *Fanum Voltumnae*, the national sanctuary of the Etruscans was located here; more historically accurate is, undoubtedly, the information given us by the historian Niccolò di Tuccia who states that the house of the painter, Lorenzo di Viterbo, who painted the *Wedding of the Virgin* in the Mazzatosta Chapel of S. Maria della Verità, was located near the Porticella.

The importance of the Church of the Trinity is due mainly to the presence of an *image of the Madonna* which was found in 1288 during restoration work ordered by a priest called Campana who was the Chaplain of Pope Nicholas V. Miraculous powers were attributed to the painting. On May 28th 1320 when the city was struck by a hurricane, the people of Viterbo were terrified; suddenly in the skies a great number of birds appeared and they must have seemed like monsters and demons come to hurl them into the flames of hell. According to a chronicler of the time, the image of "Nostra Donna nella Cappella Campana in Santo Austino sopra Faule" appeared

Sanctuary of Maria SS. Liberatrice,
one of the four statues in niches
on the façade; (right) *façade of the church*
divided into two registers
adorned with semi-columns and pilasters.

Sanctuary of Maria SS. Liberatrice,
detail of the façade.

miraculously and "by Her Grace they were liberated". After this supernatural event the image was called Maria SS. Liberatrice and an act of veneration is performed each year by the faithful who walk in a solemn procession along the streets of the neighborhood. The painting is located in a Chapel in the right nave of the church and is surrounded by numerous ex-voto objects including an extraordinary reproduction in solid silver of the city of Viterbo, which, according to the historian Feliciano Bussi weighs over fourteen pounds, and was offered in thanks by the Magistrates of the Commune.

After the miracle had taken place the church was soon overwhelmed by the crowds which thronged to see the painting, and it was deemed necessary to enlarge the building. A series of alterations was begun: in 1421 thanks to the generosity of Pope Martin V the church was restored after it had been severely damaged by fire, and in 1727 it was completely rebuilt as we see it today. The Renaissance cloister is reached through the door located on the right of the façade. This structure owes its magnificence mainly to a church restoration that never took place: in fact, the thirty-six monolithic columns which adorn it were placed there in 1514 by order of Cardinal Egidio Antonini who was then General of the Augustinian Order, but they had been prepared ten years earlier by Cardinal Fazio Santoro in

Santa Maria Liberatrice, interior, central nave (above); *main altar* (left); *detail of the dome* (below).

Prato Giardino, public park of Viterbo.

*Prato Giardino, bust of
king Vittorio Emanuele II (1878).*

order to enlarge the church. Due to the death of the Cardinal in 1510 the work was never carried out. The paintings in the church are by 17th century Mannierists and illustrate events in the *Life of Saint Augustine*. The *fountain* attached to the wall of one of the corridors would appear to be of an earlier date than the cloister. War and urban transformation have canceled every trace of the convent and the *Church of San Agostino*, of which only the name remains in a little plaza adjacent to the Sanctuary. A nearby road recalls the other name that was given to the convent, Santa Maria in Volturno, which referred to Friar Annio's fanciful theory about the location of *Fanum Voltumnae*. Up until the beginning of the 20th century the convent was occupied by Augustinian nuns who had replaced a community of Benedictine nuns, according to a document signed by Cardinal Riario and a later confirmation on the part of Pope Alexander VI.

Outside the portion of city walls which goes from Piazza della Rocca to Piazza San Faustino is the municipal park, **Prato Giardino**. This was originally called the Prato della Dogana (the Fields of the Custom house) because it was the area where merchandise in transit was sorted and checked. In the second half of the 14th century it became the gardens of the nearby Rocca, and a portion of it was used as a parade ground. From the 15th to the 17th century it belonged to various patrician families like the Gatti, Baglioni and Marsciano and in 1683 it became the property of the Chigi Montoro family. But the enjoyment of this park became an issue between the owners and the leasers (the property was frequently leased starting in the 18th century) and the city magistrates who claimed a series of privileges which had been traditionally granted to the citizens of Viterbo who were used to strolling in the park, but also for using it as a parade ground, for religious processions, and even as a pasture for animals. This conflict of interest brought about a long series legal actions until it was finally decided in 1843 that the Municipality of Viterbo would lease the land in perpetuity. In 1855 work was begun to create pathways and plant trees in the park and went on for about twenty years. The architect Virginio Vespignani was appointed in 1868 to create a monumental entrance way (the present gate which was made after the last war was designed by Rodolfo Salcini). The director of public parks in Florence, Nutini, drew up of an overall plan in 1873. The generation that had lived during the Risorgimento wished to express their enthusiasm by placing statues of its protagonists along the pathways of the park, where we can now see the busts of *Vittorio Emanuele II* (1878), of *Garibaldi* (1882) and of *Mazzini* (1891). Recently the bust of a Viterbese musician, *Cesare Dobici*, has been added. During the last war, the Prato Giardino was used extensively by military troops in transit and for this reason it was severely damaged by bombing. It has now been completely restored and is an oasis of peace even though the city has continued to expand so that what was once a garden on the edge of the city is now a green island surrounded by the buildings of the new neighborhoods which have sprung up in the meantime.

Prato Giardino, lake in the center of the park.

THE CITY OF VITERBO
AND THE ARMED FORCES

The history of the city of Viterbo after the unification of Italy is inextricably bound to that of the various branches of the armed forces which have been stationed there. At the end of the 19th century the Second Regiment of Grenadiers of Sardinia had their garrison in the city; they were followed, in the first decades of our century by the 60th Infantry, and then, in the years immediately preceding the war in Africa, 1935-36, and during the last war, by the white-trimmed uniforms of the 3rd Regiment of the Grenadiers of Sardinia mixing with the blue-gray uniforms of the aviators stationed at the Tommaso Fabbri airport which was built in those years with the intention of using it as a base for the 9th Squad of Bombardiers. During the war years, near the airport an important military center was built which became the garrison of the first Parachute divisions, the Folgore, *which had been just recently created and transferred to Viterbo from nearby Tarquinia. After the dramatic events of 1943-45, during which a vast variety of different models and colors of uniforms, soldiers of different races, nationalities and languages came and went, the Parachutists finally returned. They stayed only briefly before being permanently moved to Pisa and to Leghorn, but their bond with the city is symbolized by the monument erected in their honor in the center of the city, dedicated to the* Paracadutisti d'Italia, *designed by Paolo Caccia Dominioni, who spent years searching for the remains of the dead at El Alamein. The parachute divisions were replaced by the Gunners of the 8th* Pesante Campale *and by the* Bersaglieri *of the* Pozzuolo del Friuli *Regiment.*

Near the airport is the school for Vigilanza Aerea Militare (VAM) which trains the divisions of the Air Force that act in military police and surveillance tasks. The barracks which were originally built to house the parachutists are now the headquarters of the Army Aviation Center (C.A.E.) where pilots are trained as well as the observers who are supposed to supply strategic information to the ground troops using helicopters and small planes which can take off and land in very small spaces. The Center includes a flying field and a modern heliport.

Moreover, on the slopes of the Cimini is located the School for Non-Commissioned Infantry Officers (S.A.S), one of the most modern military installations in Europe, which trains young men who will have the difficult task of acting as a connecting link between officers and troops by offering courses in general culture as well as a specialized professional preparation.

The human side of the relationship between the city and the men of the military schools is typified by the graduation ceremonies held several times a year after each course ends, and which is called with the name of its most important ritual: the giuramento *or taking of the oath. On this occasion Viterbo is crowded with the relatives of the young men who come from every part of Italy in order to be present at the ceremony, and fill the streets and hotels creating at atmosphere of excitement and festivity in which the citizens of Viterbo also participate.*

HOT SPRINGS AND ARCHEOLOGY:
AN INTERESTING COMBINATION

The abundant hot springs found in the territory around Viterbo are due to the volcanic origin of most of the terrain in the area. One of the most important mineral water basins is located to the west of the city and its most unusual and spectacular feature may be considered the Bulicame, a sulphurous-alkaline spring whose waters gush out at 140° F., forming a tiny, almost perfectly circular lake, from which a number of streams depart like spokes from a hub and supply hot water to the thermal baths nearby. The carbon dioxide and sulphidric acid released from the water give the impression that it is boiling and the unpleasant odor and whitish incrustations which cover the hill are indications of the quantity of sulphur present in the water. This phenomenon has often excited the imagination of writers and poets: Gottifredo of Viterbo in his *Pantheon* calls the little lake the "door to Inferno", while Dante places it in his *Inferno*, comparing it to the stream he describes in the Canto XIV.

The hot springs in this hydro-mineral basin have been used for their curative powers since remotest antiquity. This is demonstrated by the presence of remains of numerous Roman villas and baths located along the portion of the Via Cassia, from which, at the locality called *delle Masse* halfway between Viterbo and Vetralla, a secondary road departed and passed along the west side of the city, running along the edge of the basin for a good distance until it reached the locality of *Aquae Passeris*, located about 3.5 miles north of Viterbo at the point where the road for Marta and Capodimonte now leave the Via Cassia.

The waters of Viterbo remained famous for their therapeutic qualities throughout the Middle Ages, and were used by Popes Gregory IX and Boniface IX. However, as an 18th century physician, Giandomenico Martelli oberved, until the 15th century there were "no Baths for public use" and the buildings, the remains of which we can see, "belonged to Private Owners who, for personal delight, as it was the custom in those times, kept similar facilities for their own use and that of their friends". In fact, even though in a document of 1259 there is mention of the purchase of buildings and springs by the city magistrates, according to Martelli, it was only in the 15th century that we have proof of the existence of "buildings belonging to the Community". These are mentioned in 1440 and are referred to as the *Bagno delle Grotte* (The Baths of the Grottoes). A few years later, after the springs had been visited several times by illustrious personages, the name was changed to Bagno del Papa (Baths of the Pope). In fact, in 1448 the mother of Pope Nicholas V visited the Baths, and two years later the pope himself arrived "to try the benefits of these waters", and, finding them "most salutary", as one who loved both magnificence and the public welfare, "he had a Palazzo built there which cost three thousand or more gold ducats". A few years later Pope Pius II was a guest in this building and, according to Martelli, "on that occasion had the Palazzo restored and enlarged". The complex took on its present day appearance about the middle of the last century, though a few alterations were made in order to modernize it around 1900. The swimming pool was built in the 1930s. During the

Fascist era the Springs became the property of the Opera Nazionale Dopolavoro and were later divided between the Municipality and INPS (the Italian pension organization), each of which created their own bathing establishment starting with radical reconstruction made necessary by the damage caused during the war.

Specialists consider the mineral waters and mud of the Viterbo basin particularly useful and for their curative powers the Springs are included among the most famous spas in Italy, especially for the treatment of arthritis, rheumatism, and respiratory diseases. The springs could potentially supply mineral water to a much larger complex of baths and could be better exploited if a "thermal spa village" were created. An important step in this direction has been taken with the recent inauguration of two bathing establishments created by the extensive remodeling of part of the pre-existing structures.

We have already mentioned the existence of Roman villas and baths built along what was once part of the Via Cassia. These, however are not the only remains of archeological interest in this area; there are in fact several Etruscan necropolises nearby, the most extensive of which is the necropolis of Castel d'Asso which is named after the site where, in the 19th century, two scholars from Viterbo, Orioli and Ceccotti, identified the Roman *Castellum Axia*, using a text in Cicero's oration "Pro Caecina", in which the exact distance of the *Castellum* is indicated – 53 miles from Rome.

Nothing remains of the ancient village except the trenches which marked its perimeter on the east side and traces of drainage ditches. It must have been a small village which was settled in the Etruscan era and subjugated by Rome when the Legions of Fabius Rulliano

*Castel d'Asso;
the Etruscan tombs with
their imposing façades in this necropolis
are situated in the cliffs on both sides
of a narrow valley where there is
an ancient road, also of Etruscan origin.*

*Castel d'Asso, Etruscan tombs
in the cliff necropolis.*

passed through the Forest of Cimina and invaded the territory. The
ruins of a castle on the cliffs overlooking the confluence of the Rio
Secco with the stream of Freddano indicate that the site was also
occupied in the Middle Ages. The castle is known to be one of the
forty-five that were subject to the jurisdiction of the Commune of
Viterbo in the 15th century. Military chronicles inform us of a battle
that never took place here in 1432, as the armies of Francesco
Sforza, positioned on a nearby plateau, awaited those of Niccolò Pic-
cinino, who seeing that he was greatly outnumbered decided to
retreat before the fight began
On the rocky face of the precipice in front of the castle and the village area, on the other side of the valley, there are the façades of the
Etruscan 'cube tombs' which make up the cliff necropolis and represent one of the most interesting examples of this kind of burial architecture. The façades we see are the front portions of tombs that are
carved into the tufa (a soft volcanic rock) and they are characteristic
of the Etruscan necropolises in some of the areas around Viterbo and
Grosseto (Norchia, S. Giuliano, Blera, Sovana). The impression they
create is majestic, with many analogies to similar structures in Asia
Minor, but, as Gargana has observed "if the similarities are infinite,
the identities lack totally".

ARTISTIC MASTERPIECES AND REMAINS
OF THE PAST IN THE ENVIRONS OF THE CITY

At the beginning of the 15th century (1414 or 1417 depending on the source) a certain Juzzante commissioned the artist Monetto to create an image of the Madonna, which was painted on a roof tile and placed among the branches of an oak in a place called Campo Graziano where Juzzante's lands were located. In the second half of the century there were rumors concerning miracles that had been worked by the sacred image, including the sudden end of the plague which had been afflicting Viterbo in 1467. The painting soon became an object of veneration and between 1470 and 1525, near the oak-tree, the **Sanctuary of the Madonna della Quercia** (Our Lady of the Oak-tree) was built, which is one of the most beautiful monuments of Renaissance Viterbo.

The Sanctuary can be reached following a tree-lined boulevard from Viterbo for slightly over a mile. The boulevard was built by order of Pope Paul III in 1540 and halfway between the city and the sanctuary there is a fountain decorated with the Lily of the Farnese family in memory of the pope who had it built, and his nephew, Cardinal Alessandro Farnese, who had it restored in 1588.

The austere and imposing façade of the Sanctuary is made of rustic stone set off by the refined decoration of the three doorways surmounted by magnificent maiolica lunettes created by Andrea della Robbia. To the side of the great stairway which leads to the church there is a massive bell-tower by Ambrogio da Milano (1480). The interior of the church is divided into three naves and has a magnificent coffered ceiling built according to designs by Antonio da Sangallo and gilded by order of Pope Paul III. The tile with the image of the Madonna, still perched on the trunk of the oak-tree is enclosed in a beautiful little tabernacle created by Andrea Bregno.

The name of the architect who designed the Sanctuary has not come down to us: the discovery of some designs by Antonio da Sangallo the Elder in the Uffizi Gallery in Florence has given the impression that he might have been the author of the original plan, and for the design of the first of the two cloisters of the adjacent convent the name of Bramante has been proposed, but for now these attributions are still hypothetical.

Passing beyond La Quercia, one soon reaches the town of **Bagnaia**, which, like La Quercia used to be a separate village but with the expansion of the city it has now become a part of Viterbo.

Bagnaia is divided into two distinct districts: the oldest is perched on top of a steep narrow hill shaped like an elongated triangle which can be reached only from the short side. Originally a castle stood on the site (which is first mentioned in a document of 963) and a village grew up around it. The accessible side was entirely blocked off by a series of fortifications: of these the only part that still exists, together with the remains of some later buildings, is the round tower next to the gate which constitutes the only access to the town.

As mentioned, **Bagnaia** is part of the municipality of Viterbo and this relationship goes very far back in time. More than eight centuries ago, in fact, in 1170 the castle, after having been the dominion of various Germanic lords, was annexed to the Commune of Viterbo, and twenty-three years later the city was appointed diocese of the

Sanctuary of Santa Maria della Quercia, façade and bell-tower by Ambrogio da Milano.

Villa Lante di Bagnaia,
Palazzina Gambara (above);
panoramic view of the gardens of the
Palazzina Gambara from the tower.

Villa Lante di Bagnaia, the fountain
called "The Cardinal's Table" with
its elongated shape was built with
wide borders so that food could be placed
on it during the banquets held in the
garden. The long pool of water in the
middle was used as a 'cooler' and directs
the gaze of the viewer toward the main
gate, the town of Bagnaia and the horizon.

Altar of the Bishop. It was in fact, the presence of the bishops which caused the *Villa*, named for the Dukes of Lante della Rovere, to be built and amplified between the 15th and 16th centuries. This family in fact leased the property around the middle of the 17th century, and the lease-hold, after being transformed and prolonged several times, was created in perpetuity by Pius IX. The villa was sold after the war to a holding company which had it carefully restored and is now the property of the Italian government. The Villa has been used for international conventions and meetings (like the recent one between the *Presidente del Consiglio*, Andreotti and the French president, Mitterrand), and has now been chosen by Prince Charles of England as a one-year school for British students doing post-graduate work in architecture.

The **Villa Lante** is one of the most handsome 16th century buildings of this type in Italy. It was completed after about a century of construction by various Bishops of Viterbo, who neglected their religious calling in order to follow their inclinations toward the appreciation of beautiful works of art and an easy, comfortable life. In the dense woodlands which grow beyond the walls of Bagnaia, up the slopes of the Cimini Hills, Bishop Raffaele Galeotto Riario created a hunting preserve and built a hunting lodge: under his successors the forest was gradually transformed into a vast park with shaded pathways connecting open spaces with elegant fountains spouting water channeled down from the nearby mountains. On one side of the park the twin Palazzos were built by Cardinal Gambara and Cardinal Montalto. The two little palazzi are connected by a series of fountains and pools which begin at the highest point of the garden and descend to the square in front of the main entrance where the coat-of-arms of the Montalto is held by the moors that the sculptor Giambologna placed in the middle of the splendid **fountain.**

It has been observed that the most singular characteristic of the Villa is the way that its three components (the stone of the buildings, the green of the vegetation and the water of the fountains) have been fused together to form a single unit which has been defined *"architettura viva"* (living architecture) which is unique and inspiring.

Villa Lante, The Quadrato Fountain with its group of Moors in the center was commissioned by Cardinal Montalto.

Villa Lante. Palazzina Gambara. The loggia with frescoes attributed to Raffaellino da Reggio and his assistants.

Detail of the Loggia. Inside the oval is a fresco attributed to Raffaellino di Reggio depicting Hercules slaying the dragon guarding the garden of the Hesperides.

San Martino al Cimino,
the Cistercian Abbey, facade.

The town of **S. Martino al Cimino**, located about 3.5 miles from Viterbo, is another place which offers sites of considerable historical interest for the visitor. The oldest of these is the majestic 13th century Cistercian Abbey overlooking the town. A little church, probably standing farther down the valley than the present day one, was donated by a certain Benedetto son of Auperto, to Siccardo, Abbott of Farfa in 830; this was the origin of the monastic community of San Martino, which was first occupied by monks of the Benedictine order and later, in 1150, by the Cistercians when Pope Eugene III had a group of monks transferred from the convent of San Suplizio in Savoy. In the beginning of the 13th century the Abbey was acquired by a colony of Cistercian monks coming from the French monastery of Pontigny; the magnificent abbey was built in this era, by order of the Viterbese Cardinal Raniero Capocci. Though little remains of the monastery, just a small portion of the cloister and a few rooms, including the one which is called the Monk's Hall, the Church is still almost completely intact. The three naves present the main characteristics of the Cistercian Gothic style with their cross-vaults and prominent ribs supporting the high ceilings. The pentagonal apse is unusual though examples exist in some French churches (this is probably due to the fact that the abbey depended on the French monastery at Pontigny). The great windows of the façade were built later, in the 15th century, to replace the original rose-window and the twin bell-towers were built between 1651 and 1654, mostly in order to brace up the massive façade which was ill supported by the unsteady terrain of the plaza. After having its moment of glory in the second half of the 13th century during the papacy of

San Martino al Cimino,
one of the access gates to the village.

Gregory X. the monastery slowly declined and was eventually abandoned by the monks; it became a commendam of various cardinals and finally in 1564, when the last commendatary, Ranuccio Farnese, forfeited it, it became part of the Capitular Altar of the Vatican Basilica of St. Peter's. In 1645 pope Innocent X. through an exchange, created San Martino a principality and elevated his sister-in-law, Lady Olimpia Maidalchini Pamphilj to the rank of princess. The other most interesting aspect of this little center is the town planning, which came about in this era, and is considered a model of 17th century urban organization with its unique oblong plan, which is clearly visible from above, and for the singular way in which the little row houses are arranged against the city walls. Next to the Abbey is located the huge structure of the **Palazzo Doria-Pamphilj** which was originally just an annex of the monastery which had undergone major transformations in the second half of the 15th century before Lady Olimpia turned it into her lavish residence. The building was acquired by the Provincial Tourist Board of Viterbo, who now have their offices in it, with the intent of using it as a convention center.

In 1172 the Viterbese, exasperated by a long series of hostile acts and betrayals perpetrated by their unfriendly neighbors, decided to find a radical and definitive solution to their difficult relations with the

Cistercian Abbey, interior.

Ferento, the city declined in the first centuries of the Middle Ages and was finally destroyed by the Viterbese in 1172.

town of **Ferento**. By this time very little remained of the city which had been both large and important in Roman times. It had been devastated by barbarian incursions throughout the early Middle Ages and was just a large *borgo* or village which the attacking army had no trouble in destroying, reducing it in short order to a mass of rubble and forcing the inhabitants to move elsewhere. Afterwards some of the people of Ferento moved into caves in the nearby cliffs and a new village was formed whose name recalls its distant origins, Grotte S. Stefano (Caves of St. Stephen), while others (according to tradition, only the richest people, which the Viterbese envisioned as new tax-payers) settled in the city of the victors and created a new neighborhood which was called San Faustino.

The ruins of **Ferento** are located about five miles from Viterbo. The city had Etruscan origins but became important only during the era of Imperial Rome. There are inscriptions which tend to indicate that the Emperor Otto was born there. Excavations have been conducted here since the beginning of the 20th century; among the most interesting discoveries has been the **Roman Theatre** which has been recently restored so that it can be used for many different types of entertainment: ancient dramas, opera, ballet, theatre and pop music recitals. Near the theatre along the road covered with paving stones there are remains of houses, of the baths and a church which was built in Ferento in the early Middle Ages. About a half mile away, archeological excavations have uncovered an Etruscan village.

The nearby city of **Orvieto**, unlike Viterbo which is in Latium, is in Umbria; it is built on top of a tufa plateau and has extremely ancient origins. In the Etruscan era it can probably be identified with the city of *Volsinii Veteres*. There are many interesting remains from this

Ferento, Roman theatre.

On this page and opposite: ***the Roman theatre at Ferento.***

Opposite: ***Orvieto, façade of the Cathedral.***

period: the **Necropolis del Crocifisso del Tufo**, various tombs and temples. There are also many important Medieval monuments in Orvieto: **the Basilica of Saints Andrew and Bartholomew**, the **Abbey of Saints Severo and Martiro**. The earliest structures of the **Church of San Giovenale** were built sometime before the 10th century. Orvieto flourished in the Middle Ages and the skyline of city still bristles with the numerous tower-houses typical of this era. The 12th-13th century **Palazzo del Popolo** is also worth a visit.

The city is dominated by the magnificent Cathedral, an architectural masterpiece of extraordinary beauty, the construction of which lasted from the 13th until the end of the 16th century and engaged some of the most illustrious artists of the time: Arnolfo di Cambio, who was probably responsible for the original Romanesque design, Lorenzo Maitani who completed it and designed the wonderful Gothic façade, Andrea Pisano, Orcagna, Ippolito Scalza and Raffaele da Montelupo. Inside the Cathedral the visitor may admire the Chapel of San Brizio with frescoes by Beato Angelico and Luca Signorelli (15th-16th century); the frescoes in the apse by Ugolino di Prete Ilario (14th century); a fresco by Gentile da Fabriano; a reliquiary by Ugolino di Vieri (14th century).

Orvieto is also famous for the **Pozzo di San Patrizio** (St. Patrick's well) built in the 16th century by Antonio da Sangallo the Younger in order to assure a water supply to the city in case of siege.

The town of **Bolsena** is located on the slopes of the crater of the Volsini mountains and extends down to the plains below, on the

Orvieto, panorama of the city.

Bolsena, view of the Medieval quarter.

Bolsena, the Bisentina island at sunset.

northeast shore of the lake of the same name. the *Lago di Bolsena*, at 1140 ft. above sea level.

This picturesque village takes it name from the **Rocca** or fortress at the top of the hill in the Medieval quarter. Inside of the castle there is a museum, the *Museo Territoriale di Bolsena*, which is divided into six sections which illustrate the history of the lake and of the different civilizations which have arisen and developed on its shores.

Well worth a visit, is the **Basilica of Santa Cristina**, an architectural complex which is divided into four distinct units: the little hypogeum basilica called the Grotto of Santa Cristina (a hypogeum is an underground burial chamber) and the catacombs, the Romanesque building with three naves, the Chapel of the Miracle, and the Chapel of St. Lawrence. The façade of the Romanesque church is 15th century and was built by Cardinal Giovanni dei Medici. later pope Leone X. It is divided into three parts with elegant decorations on the pilaster faces, the continuity of which is interrupted by a trapezoid shaped entablature. Two maiolica lunettes attributed to the Florentine, Buglioni, surmount the main door of the church. The slender and elegant bell-tower, adorned with three orders of biforus windows, was built in the 13th century.

Bolsena is also famous for its folklore, like the manifestation of the *Infiorata* celebrated in occasion of the feast of Corpus Domini, and the representation of the *Mysteries*, perhaps the most important from a cultural and historical point of view.

*Bolsena, view of the fortress,
the Rocca Monaldeschi della Cervara,
now the Museum of the Territory* (above);
detail of the Medieval fortress (left).

Next page: *Bolsena,
Basilica of Santa Cristina.*

INDEX OF THE ITINERARIES

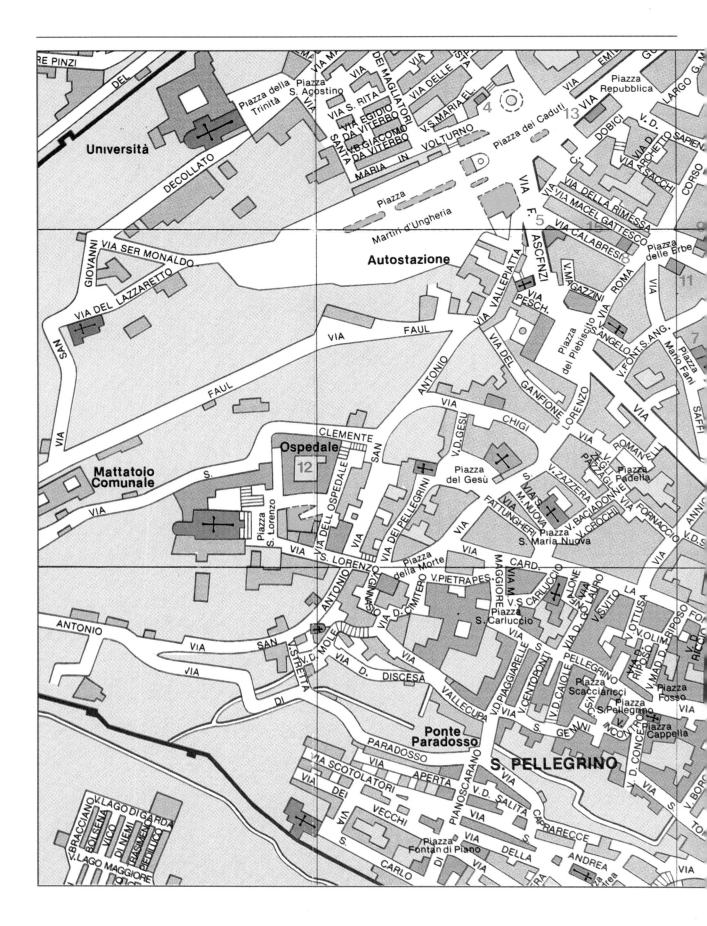

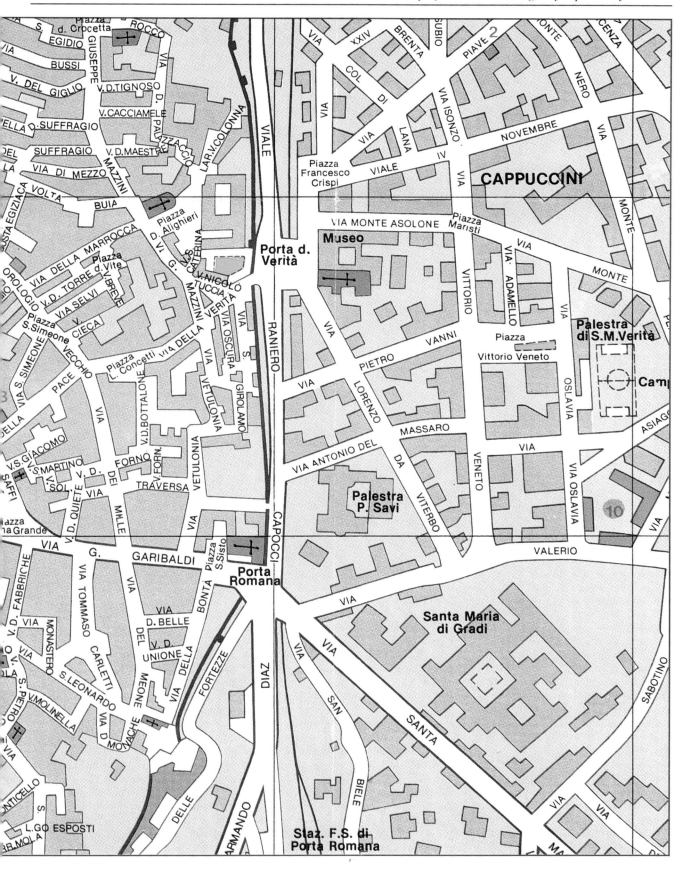